Adventure Cycling™ in
Northern California

Selected On & Off Road Rides

Adventure Cycling™ in

Northern California

Selected On & Off Road Rides

The Adventure Cycling Association

THE
MOUNTAINEERS

Published by
The Mountaineers
1001 SW Klickitat Way
Seattle, WA 98134

The Adventure Cycling Association
150 E. Pine Street
Missoula, MT 59807-8303

10 9 8 7
5 4 3 2 1

Published simultaneously in Great Britain by Cordee, 3a DeMontfort Street, Leicester, England, LE1 7HD

Manufactured in the United States of America

Edited by Sarah Lane
Maps by The Adventure Cycling Association
Cover design by Amy Peppler Adams, designLab—Seattle
Book design by Alice Merrill

Cover photograph: © Gregg Adams Photography
Frontispiece: The descent will have you grinning from ear to ear. (photo by Jim Haagen-Smit)

Library of Congress Cataloging-in-Publication Data
Adventure cycling in northern California : selected on- and off-road rides / the
    Adventure Cycling Association.
        p.   cm.
    Includes index.
    ISBN 0-89886-504-2
    1. All terrain cycling—California, Northern—Guidebooks. 2. California,
Northern—Guidebooks. I. Adventure Cycling Association.
GV1045.5.C22C252   1997
796.6'3'09794—dc21   96–47852
                                                                         CIP

♻ Printed on recycled paper

Table of Contents

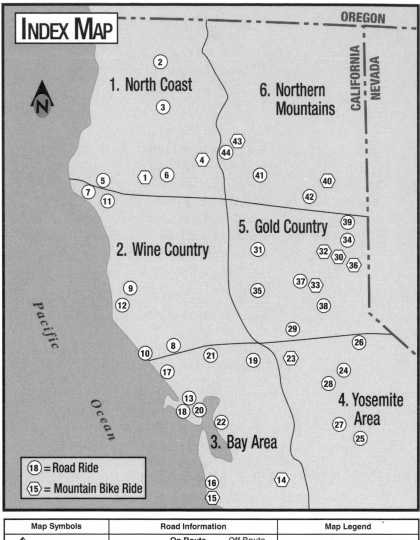

INDEX MAP

OREGON

CALIFORNIA NEVADA

N

②

1. North Coast

③

6. Northern Mountains

43
44

④

⑤ ① ⑥
⑦
⑪

41

40

42

2. Wine Country

5. Gold Country

39
34

31

32 30
36

⑨

37 33

⑫

35

38

⑩ ⑧
⑰

29

21

19

23

26

24
28

13
18 20

22

4. Yosemite Area

27
25

3. Bay Area

14

⑱ = Road Ride
⑮ = Mountain Bike Ride

16
15

Pacific

Ocean

Map Symbols		Road Information			Map Legend	
⌂	Ride Beginning Point		**On Route**	**Off Route**	*Creeks*	
↖	Direction Arrow	Limited Access Highway	⑮ ⑫	⑮ ⑫		Dam
★	Route turn	Federal Highway	⑫	⑫	*Rivers, Lakes*	
✛	Peaks and Elevations				Major Park Boundary	
■	Points of Interest	State Highway	⑲	⑲		
○	City Center	County Road	653	653	**COUNTY LINE**	
▢	Highway Interchange	Gravel Road			**STATE LINE**	
△	Campground Location	Trail			Railroad Tracks	
☷	Picnic Table Location					

Preface

The rides in this book were submitted by members of the Adventure Cycling Association, a national association of over 40,000 individuals who love using their bicycles for exploration, discovery, and adventure. Based in Missoula, Montana, Adventure Cycling has for more than twenty years mapped the back roads of the United States expressly for cyclists and has created and helped maintain a national network of bicycling "highways."

Many cyclists do not have the weeks or months required to undertake the long-distance, coast-to-coast routes that Adventure Cycling has created. There is a need for many shorter, quality rides that cyclists can complete in a day, a weekend, or a short vacation. One of the aims of this book is to provide cyclists with information about such rides.

Bicycling continues to be one of the fastest-growing activities in the country. The well-known rides—especially those near urban areas—are attracting more and more cyclists every year, yet thousands of miles of good riding, both on and off pavement, go virtually unused. Another aim of this book is to identify excellent but little-known cycling opportunities. In directing cycling enthusiasts to new routes, we hope to reduce cycling traffic on well-known trails.

To compose this guide, we asked our members to nominate their favorite rides in northern California. Each contributing member has ridden the trail he or she described and collected the route information along with accommodation listings, ideas about what to see and do, and special notes about the ride. You can read about the contributing cyclists in the About the Authors section at the back of the book.

The Mountaineers Books of Seattle has entered into the project as a partner to produce and distribute this series of great cycling destinations.

Maps for the book were prepared by the Adventure Cycling staff based on information supplied by the contributors. Keep in mind that recent road or trail construction—or natural phenomena—may have changed the trails somewhat since the descriptions were written. For this reason, when appropriate, we have listed other maps and information sources to supplement the maps in the book.

We have worked hard to provide a wide variety of tours, including rides suitable for cyclists of all skill levels. Rides range from a few hours to several days, and the descriptions specify whether they are appropriate for road bikes or mountain bikes.

Follow the signs to the trail. (photo by William Paxson)

Acknowledgments

We want to thank the members of the Adventure Cycling Association who submitted their favorite rides for our consideration. There were many fine rides offered that could not be included in this volume.

Several people on the Adventure Cycling staff were involved with the production of this book:

- Tom Robertson, our cartography department assistant, did the lion's share of collecting the routes from members, reviewing the rides, and assembling the final selection with input from other staff members. Tom completed a lot of the work on the maps, corrected galleys and page proofs, and worked closely with the publisher to make the maps and text consistent and accurate.

- Carla Majernik, director of the cartography department, developed the mapping approach and designed the initial templates that were used in the production of the maps. The final product—clean, readable, and useful—is what we have come to expect from Carla in her twenty-plus years of developing maps for Adventure Cycling.

- Gary MacFadden, executive director at Adventure Cycling, compiled the narrative text supplied by members and wrote the introductory material for the book. Gary loves both on- and off-pavement riding and was itching to get some use out of his journalism degree.

We also want to acknowledge the outstanding work done by Sarah Lane, editor of this book. It is through her efforts that a rough manuscript was transformed into a usable, readable book. Our thanks also to the staff at The Mountaineers Books for their professional handling of this project.

Introduction

HISTORY

The settlement of California is closely tied to a legend that became a reality, or, as in the movies that are spawned in the southern reaches of the state, at least a facsimile of reality. The early explorers—Cortés, Bodega, Drake—came to California seeking the fabled treasures of El Dorado, where riches were rumored to lie about, waiting to be plucked from the ground.

In 1510, a Spanish romance writer, García Ordoñez de Montalvo, further fanned the fires of greed in the fictional Las Sergas de Esplandián, in which he told of the wonders of an island paradise called California, where precious gems and gold lay about for the taking. Small wonder that California was the name Cortés and his crew bestowed on the land when they first saw it in 1535, even if the jewels were not immediately apparent.

Many followed—Spanish conquistadors and English pirates bobbed along the coastline in their galleons, seeking the bays that would take them to the elusive riches. The Spanish established a chain of twenty-one missions between what would become San Diego and Sonoma, along the Camino Real (the Royal Road). Over the decades, the new land was visited, explored, exploited, and at various times claimed by English, French, Americans, Spanish, Russians, and Mexicans.

Gold remained hidden from view until the mid-1800s. When it was at long last discovered, it was not by explorers or pirates or conquistadors or even a regiment of American soldiers. The discovery was made by a lone carpenter building a mill on the American River near the present site of Sacramento.

When James Marshall plucked the flecks of shiny yellow metal from the mill's tailrace on a blustery day in January 1848, he had no cause to believe that his discovery at Sutter's Mill would forever change the natural face, the politics, the very fabric of this new land. During the following two decades, thousands of treasure seekers swarmed into California in search of easy riches and a better life. Some found what they sought, but many more found only discouragement. Still, new gold seekers arrived. The population of northern California blossomed; in only two years, San Francisco mushroomed from a population of only 500 in 1848 to a thriving metropolis of more than 20,000. Political power quickly shifted away from Los Angeles, at the time a sleepy little trading village. The stage was set for a regional rivalry that continues today.

If political separatists had had their way, you might be getting ready to sample some bicycle rides in the state of Northern California, or perhaps Jefferson State. The notion of splitting California into two (or more) states has been introduced at least twenty times since the state was inducted into the Union. As early as 1851, Los Angeles politicians, jealous of San Francisco's rise in political strength, proposed carving a second state out of the southern portion of California. The proposed new name? Colorado. The advent of the Civil War put the state-splitting agenda aside but only temporarily. By the time the two sides got back to arguing, the proposed new name had already been taken.

In the late 1930s, northern Californians led another cry to split the state, this time wanting to create the new state of Jefferson. Again war interceded, with the bombing of Pearl Harbor.

Is the regional bickering over? Not by a long shot. In 1992, separatists in northern California forced onto a ballot a test measure to split the state. In the final tally, twenty-seven out of the thirty-one counties voted for the split. In 1993, legislation was introduced to divide California into not two but three states (northern, central, and southern).

It appears the regional bickering may continue. Ideally, it will not take a war to distract the separatists this time.

GEOGRAPHY

As the third largest of the United States, California covers some latitude as well as longitude. With just over 158,000 square miles, the state boasts a wider variety of climates and topography than any other state—from lush rain forest to barren desert, ice-carved peaks to fertile agricultural valleys. The 1,265-mile coastline represents just less than 10 percent of all the coastline in the contiguous United States. The bend in the coastline is so radical that, were you to cycle from Reno, Nevada, to the coastal metropolis of San Diego, you would actually have to travel east. Yet Eureka, also on the coast in northern California, is the most western of West Coast cities.

Look closely for the bike on the hill. (photo by Gary MacFadden)

We will explore cycling opportunities in the northern third of the state, traversing the Sierra and Coast Ranges, the Northern Mountains, the Central Valley, and the narrow coastal lowlands. In this book, northern California has been broken into six smaller regions: the North Coast, the Wine Country, the Bay Area (San Francisco and environs), the Yosemite Area, the Gold Country, and the Northern Mountains. For each of the six regions, you will find a choice of road and mountain bike rides, encompassing a range of riding abilities as well as a variety of experiences. What follows is a quick overview of each region.

Region 1: North Coast

The North Coast is noted for its fog and rugged coastlines. However, perhaps the best known of all the scenic wonders in this region are the beautiful forests of tall coastal redwoods. The oldest of these trees are at least 2,200 years old; the tallest attain heights of 368 feet.

Region 2: Wine Country

The north central coast is dominated by the "Avenue of the Giants" to the north and the famed Wine Country to the south. The "Avenue of the Giants" is the 33-mile old highway that winds through some of the largest remaining stands of redwoods in the region. The inland valleys of Napa, Sonoma, Mendocino, and Lake Counties are known as California's wine country, despite the fact that only about 20 percent of California wines are produced here.

Region 3: Bay Area

The Bay Area is made up of all the communities up and down the bay from San Francisco. In addition to these urban centers, the Bay Area offers its own wilderness and wayside pleasures. The Point Reyes National Seashore, just a few miles north of San Francisco, is a good example, encompassing 5,000 acres of fog-shrouded lagoons, lowland marshes, sandy beaches, and ridge-top forests. However, the best-known feature of this region is the Golden Gate Bridge, which was completed in 1937. This bright red-orange pathway up to the fog not only spans the entrance to the San Francisco Bay, but links the city to some popular recreation areas in the north.

Region 4: Yosemite Area

This region encompasses geographic diversity remarkable for an area its size. From the Sacramento Valley region to the Gold Country to a portion of the Sierra Nevada, there is a little terrain here for everyone's tastes. Dominating this region is Yosemite National Park, a wonder of granite, gorges, and well-known peaks. Yosemite is quite a contrast to the lush Sacramento Valley, part of the 400-mile-long Central Valley.

Region 5: Gold Country

When gold was first discovered on the American River, hundreds of thousands of fortune hunters set out for California. People still flock to the Gold Country today but more for recreational than economical pursuits. The area is something of a mecca for snow and water skiing, hiking, biking, and camping. Mark Twain, who once lived there, wrote about the area, "Three months of camp life on Lake Tahoe would restore an Egyptian mummy to his pristine vigor, and give him an appetite like an alligator."

Region 6: Northern Mountains

The northern mountains are characterized by mountain peaks under cobalt blue skies, rushing rivers, crystal-clear lakes, and meadows full of blooming wildflowers during the short summers. The area is generally too far north for most travelers' tastes, which makes it the perfect spot for cyclists looking to get away from crowds. If you keep your eyes peeled, you might catch a glimpse of Bigfoot, the legendary 600-pound man-ape, who is spotted in this region from time to time.

WHERE THIS GUIDE WILL (AND WILL NOT) TAKE YOU

The rides—especially those in the off-road category—meet two conditions. First, they will not take you across private land. While some landowners are willing to let bicyclists cross their land, many are not. Second, they will not take you into wilderness areas. The Wilderness Act of 1964 described wilderness as closed to "any means of mechanical conveyance." Some bicyclists argue that the bicycle does far less harm to trails than do mules or pack horses, which typically are allowed in wilderness areas. This is not the forum for a discussion about the

Wilderness Act and its effect on cycling. This book's recommendations adhere to the current law, good or bad, because there is a lot of great cycling to be had out there without bending or breaking the rules.

DIFFICULTY RATING

No one has yet devised the perfect rating system for bicycle rides. The problem is that no two cyclists are exactly alike. What is difficult for one rider may be another cyclist's typical "tune-up" ride.

To address this ambiguity, we asked each contributor to clearly describe the route, the pavement or trail condition, and the number and severity of climbs. Then we asked them to rate the rides as Easy, Moderate, or Difficult. After reviewing the rides, in most cases we agreed with the opinions of the contributors. In a few cases we upgraded the level of difficulty.

The rides in the Easy class are short and fairly flat with few (if any) hills. These rides should be fine for novice cyclists or families with younger riders. In the Moderate category, rides will generally include some steep hills or at least rolling hills. Some otherwise flat tours may be rated as Moderate only because they extend over two or more days. Rides in the Hard category may very well involve dismounting to walk up steep grades or to get around large rocks or fallen trees. This last category generally includes the rides with the most climbing.

COURTESY

In the past half-dozen years, mountain bike sales have exploded. (As of this writing, they account for nine out of every ten bicycles sold to adults.) While most mountain bikers never leave the pavement, the number of people venturing into the backcountry on these capable bicycles is growing, as are conflicts with the more traditional users of hiking trails. Observe some extra courtesies when bicycling the backcountry. Courtesy comes down to riding with the attitude that you are sharing the road or trail with other users, whether car and truck drivers, hikers, equestrians, or other cyclists. The following list of guidelines was developed by the Adventure Cycling Association:

1. Stay on the designated travel corridor and off the vegetation.
2. Yield right-of-way to slower and less mechanized users.
3. Do not cut ruts: Keep off muddy roads and trails.
4. Police your speed and ride in control.

Please try to stay on the trail. (photo by Jim Haagen-Smit)

5. Respect trail closures and no-trespassing signs.
6. Leave gates as you found them.
7. Practice minimum-impact travel and camping.
8. Help teach new riders proper trail etiquette.

CLOTHING

Weight and bulk, versatility, and suitability for anticipated conditions are the primary considerations when you are deciding what goes along on your ride. It is important that clothing not restrict your arms and legs, as the constant motion of pedaling can cause terrific irritation. Shirts and shorts for summer riding give more freedom of movement. When the temperatures drop, switch to long warm-up pants or tights (not jeans) and a windbreaker of breathable, waterproof material. Pay special attention to keeping your knee joints warm; they often stiffen easily in chilly weather or during long downhills.

Possibly the most important investment that you can make in clothing for cycling is what you choose for cycling shorts. Anyone who has experienced a sore behind due to binding underwear or knotting shorts can attest to the importance of having the right shorts. What determines what type of shorts are right for you varies considerably according to style, body shape, and weight. Check them out around town before heading off for a three-day tour!

On colder days it is preferable to have several layers of light clothing that can be removed or replaced as the temperatures fluctuate. Blue jeans and sweat pants are not appropriate riding attire: Jeans have bulky seams in all the wrong places, and both types of clothing are moisture magnets.

If you are wearing only one layer of warm clothes, you are out of luck if the weather suddenly warms, or if you begin to perspire from the cycling activity. A layer of polypropylene next to the body works great for wicking moisture away. (On some people, polypro causes an uncomfortable rash. Check it out before you begin an extended ride.)

Cycling shoes are another investment that you might be wise to make if you expect to be doing a lot of cycling. Talk with the people at your bicycle shop about the types of riding you intend to be doing. Some shoes have the pedal attachment built right into the soles; others depend on toe clips and straps to keep the foot correctly situated on the pedal. Many people ride in comfort for years in good-quality athletic shoes and never bother to purchase special cycling shoes. It all depends upon your style of riding.

YOUR BICYCLE

Bicycles nowadays come in a dizzying array of types, each meant for one of two specific types of riding: on road or off road. These types are further divided into road racing, hybrid, touring, competition, commuting, club ride, and a few more. You will enjoy the tours included in this book a lot more if you have the right type of bicycle for the type of riding you will be doing.

If you already have a bicycle, match your tours to the bike. If you are shopping for a bike, figure out in advance what type of riding you most want to do. Then get yourself to a bicycle shop (not a general merchandise discount store) and purchase a bicycle that will take you on the types of rides that most interest you.

Wheels and Tires

Another item you will want to carefully consider is tires—where the rubber meets the road (or trail, as the case may be). To escape specific import duties and to give potential buyers a sprightly ride around the parking lot, most manufacturers put narrow tires on their bicycles.

The majority of mountain bikes as delivered to shops are equipped with 1.5-inch tires. These are too small for tours or even day rides off road, although they will probably hold up nicely for Sunday rides on the local rail-trail. If you are planning to head off road—and you probably are or you would not be reading this book—you will need tires in the 1.9- to 2.5-inch range.

On road bikes, the builders really go narrow on the tires—it seems everyone wants to be Greg LeMond. While narrow tires offer less rolling resistance, they are much more easily damaged, and the time you save by going fast will be lost in patching tires from rim cuts. For on-road riding, you will do much better with 1.25-inch tires, which are available for both the 27" and 700C rims. Make sure when swapping wheel and tire combinations that the rubber still clears the frame's brake bridges and fenders (if installed) and that the brake blocks still contact the rim and not the tire sidewalls.

SAFETY

Safety should be a primary concern for all bicyclists, especially when heading for the backcountry where they might have difficulty getting help in the event of a problem. The first safety recommendation is that you tell a friend when and where you will be riding and when you expect to return. That way, if you run into trouble, at least you will be reassured that someone back at home will be wondering where you are and will be able to get you help if you need it.

Bicycle Maintenance and Condition

Keeping your bicycle in good mechanical condition is key in riding safety. Check it each time you go riding, especially after any disassembly, such as after removing a front wheel to install the bike in a car-top carrier. Maybe you put the quick-release skewer back on, but did you remember to reconnect the front brake hanger?

Here is a quick mechanical condition checklist:
- Do the brake pads contact the rim properly when closed?
- Are the rims true?
- Are the cables intact, without fraying?
- Are tires inflated correctly for the riding conditions you will experience?
- Are all of the spokes intact?
- Do the wheel hubs turn smoothly?

Nicasio School (photo by Emmett Maguire)

- Are the handlebars adjusted correctly and locked in position?
- Is the seat adjusted to let you pedal efficiently but are at least 2 inches of seat post still installed in the seat tube?
- Is the seat post locked into position?
- Are the pedals secure on the crank arms?
- Are the toe clips (if you are using them) in good condition?
- Is the chain lubricated?
- Are the front and rear derailleurs working correctly? Are they both tightly attached to the frame?

A quick bicycle check only takes moments before each ride, but it can pay big dividends in safe and enjoyable cycling.

The Helmet

The first piece of safety equipment for all bicyclists, whether on or off road, is a good-quality cycling helmet. Wearing a helmet has nothing to do with riding abilities. A skilled cyclist with lightning-fast reflexes can be downed by a stick, a pavement groove, or even a patch of slippery pine needles. When you start heading down is not the time to wish you had a helmet on your head.

22

A small rearview mirror that attaches to the helmet is also a good investment for riding on a shared-roadway route (sharing with automobiles, that is). Any early indication of traffic approaching from behind is a good safety booster.

Sunglasses

Sunglasses or goggles are another good safety accessory. They improve your vision by cutting glare in bright weather, they keep rain and bugs out of your eyes, especially on descents, and they reduce or eliminate tearing in your eyes from wind.

Visibility

When cycling on shared-roadway routes in the car-bicycle mix, visibility becomes a prime safety factor. Consider bright-colored clothing, reflective flags, and/or safety triangles (fanny bumpers) as standard equipment, not accessories.

Road and Trail Sense

Practice safe cycling habits, whether on a shared-roadway route or on a backcountry trail. On roads, ride as close to the right as practical, depending upon the condition of the shoulders or riding lane and obstructions such as debris or parked cars. You might even pull off the roadway at times to ease the flow of traffic, especially if you get a nervous driver behind you who does not want to pass you and begins to back up traffic.

Pulling off the road or waving cars around you are examples of defensive cycling, an approach to biking that involves anticipating how road conditions and road users will affect your safety. Planning routes and cycling times is also a part of defensive cycling. Cycling at dusk may be very pleasant, but driver fatigue and dwindling light make this one of the most dangerous times to be on a shared roadway. In contrast, early morning is one of the best times for safe bicycling; traffic is usually light, and visibility is better.

Do not just anticipate problems from automobile drivers—hundreds of accidents each year involve cyclists running into other cyclists, when riding in a closely spaced pack and plowing into each other. On busy roads, keep your bicycles spaced at least two bike-lengths apart and ride in a single line. On less busy roads, it is tempting to ride side by side for a pleasant chat with your cycling partner, but only do this if the sight distance is long enough and you are visible to approaching drivers from both directions. If the road is curvy and/or hilly, ride single file and schedule more frequent stops for the chatting.

Speaking of stopping, get all of the way off the road or trail when taking a break. Different road and trail users travel at different speeds. If a cyclist comes hurtling around a corner on a downhill run and you are standing in the trail chatting with a hiker, you are likely to get injured.

Weather

The western portion of California has a mostly marine-influenced climate, but other portions of the state can vary tremendously in weather patterns.

The general rule when bicycling is be prepared for just about anything at any time of the year. If you have chosen your light layers of clothing correctly, you will have few problems.

Keep on the lookout for wet weather, especially while cycling at higher elevations. You always face the potential of hypothermia, a condition in which the body's internal temperature has dropped below normal and that can lead to mental and physical collapse. Bicycling in wet conditions is a nearly perfect recipe for brewing hypothermia, which is brought on by exposure to cold and aggravated by wind, exhaustion, and soaking through either perspiration or condensation.

Hypothermia advances in two steps. The first is exposure and exhaustion. The moment your body begins to lose heat more quickly than it can produce it, you are suffering from exposure. Your body begins to make involuntary adjustments to preserve normal temperatures for the internal organs and you may take some voluntary steps as well, riding faster or stopping and jumping up and down or doing other exercises to try to get warm. However, this exercise will only prolong and increase the exposure.

At the second stage of hypothermia, your energy reserves are exhausted. The cold reaches your brain stem and eventually the brain itself, depriving you of your ability to reason or make judgments. You will lose control of your feet and hands, which—if you are still bicycling— will put you in a very precarious situation. If the hypothermia is untreated, your body temperature will continue to cycle down, leading to collapse and finally death.

The only way to guard against hypothermia is to stay dry. Wool has long been a popular material for bicycling clothes because, even when wet, it retains much of its insulating qualities—much better than do cotton and most synthetics. However, do not trust your clothing to do the entire job. You can get hypothermia even when swaddled from head to foot in wool, if it gets wet enough. Your best front-line protection is a good set of rain gear, including a jacket with a hood, pants, and shoe covers.

BEING PREPARED
Generations of Boy Scouts have survived scrapes in the outback by following the simple rule of "Be Prepared." It works great for cyclists, too. Preparation for the rides in this book falls into three categories: 1) bicycle tools and parts, 2) first-aid supplies, and 3) survival supplies.

Bicycle Tools and Parts
The trick is to take what you might really need in order to get out of a scrape, without taking the whole workbench. Sooner or later, you are going to need to make an adjustment to a clattering derailleur, replace a bolt, or at least fix a flat tire. Here is a list of basic tools and parts to carry on any outing. They can all fit into a small repair kit that hangs under the saddle or fits in a pocket of a handlebar bag:
- adjustable wrench (6- to 8-inch)
- slotted and Phillips screwdrivers
- nesting tire irons (the three-to-a-set plastic ones work well)
- bicycle tube repair kit
- spoke wrench
- any Allen wrenches suitable for your bicycle
- roll of electrician's tape
- some bike grease (old plastic film canisters work great to hold grease)
- chain tool
- chain lubricant (much lighter than grease)
- small cleaning rag

You should also have the following parts in your repair kit:
- spare tube to fit your tire
- rear brake cable (can be shortened to fit the front brake in an emergency)

- rear derailleur cable (can be shortened to fit the front brake in an emergency)
- some extra spokes (three for the freewheel side, three for the opposite side)
- extra chain links (do not bother with these if you decide not to carry the chain tool)
- small freezer bag with an assortment of small nuts, bolts, and washers for racks, brake attachments, water bottle cages, etc.

First-Aid Supplies

Here is another area of preparation in which you can quickly get carried away. The idea is to have just enough to treat the likely cuts, bumps, and bruises that occur on any outing or even at the backyard barbecue. Your first-aid kit should include the following:

- sunscreen
- moleskin for blisters
- antibacterial ointment
- 3-inch elastic bandage
- 2-inch roll of gauze
- two triangular bandages
- "second-skin" for burns or road rash
- baking soda for insect bites
- needles and thread
- single-edged razor blade in a blade protector
- insect repellent
- aspirin
- tweezers

Survival Supplies

The survival supplies you will need when biking are the Ten Essentials:
1. waterproof matches or butane lighter
2. compass and map of the area
3. pocketknife
4. extra water
5. extra food
6. rain gear and warm clothing
7. flashlight or headlamp

View of Hoffman Bluff (photo by John Stein)

8. plastic whistle
9. sunglasses
10. "space" (foil) blanket for body-heat retention

To the Ten Essentials, you might want to add water purification tablets. Please note, however, that you should make use of water from mountain lakes or streams only in an emergency. Water from streams and lakes can, unfortunately, make you very sick. An invisible waterborne parasite called *Giardia lamblia* can make you wish you had never gone bicycling. In advanced cases, it can make you wish you had never been born. You get giardiasis when you ingest a dormant cyst form of this parasite that can live for two to three months in water as cold as 40 degrees Fahrenheit. Many people have the notion that giardiasis is caused by livestock and that if they are high enough above where cattle might be roaming, the water is safe to drink. Not true. Giardiasis can be spread by the droppings of horses, squirrels, dogs, cats, beavers, elk, rabbits, deer, and people. In fact, some backcountry studies have suggested that humans may be the most common spreaders of Giardia cysts, simply through their improper disposal of human waste.

If you do choose to drink the water from lakes or streams and are smart enough to purify it with water tablets first, do not congratulate yourself too soon on escaping the risk of giardiasis. The cysts can take between three days and four weeks to activate in your intestines. If they do, get ready for severe diarrhea, weight loss, fatigue, the sweats, and cramps. Call a doctor if you spot the symptoms, and 'fess up to your activities. Drink plenty of fluids but avoid dairy products, which will only worsen your symptoms. There are no well-known home remedies and even the medically prescribed treatments can have unpleasant side effects.

Now, if a refreshing drink from a mountain lake or stream still seems worth all that potential upheaval, all we can do is wish you good luck.

A NOTE ABOUT SAFETY

Safety is an important concern in all outdoor activities. No guidebook can alert you to every hazard or anticipate the limitations of every reader. Therefore, the descriptions of roads, trails, routes, and natural features in this book are not representations that a particular place or excursion will be safe for your party. When you follow any of the routes described in this book, you assume responsibility for your own safety. Under normal conditions, such excursions require the usual attention to traffic, road and trail conditions, weather, terrain, the capabilities of your party, and other factors. Because many of the lands in this book are subject to development and/or change of ownership, conditions may have changed since this book was written that make your use of some of these routes unwise. Always check for current conditions, obey posted private property signs, and avoid confrontations with property owners or managers. Keeping informed on current conditions and exercising common sense are the keys to a safe, enjoyable outing.

—*The Mountaineers*

Region 1

North Coast

A "thermal" break along the route (photo by Allen Kost)

South Fork Trail

Submitted by John Stein

This historic mining trail winds along the South Fork of the Trinity River through oak and pine forests to Smoky Creek. A few short hills make this mountain bike trail in the South Fork National Recreation Area an easy ride.

Type of ride: mountain bike
Starting point: Hellgate Campground Trailhead parking area, near Forest Glen
Finishing point: same
Distance: 14.6 miles round trip
Level of difficulty: easy
General terrain: follows river grade with some steep, short pitches
Traffic conditions: nearly nonexistent; some four-wheel-drive vehicles on lower route segment
Estimated riding time: 2 to 3 hours
Best season/time of day to ride: trail maintained in June; snow free for most of the year

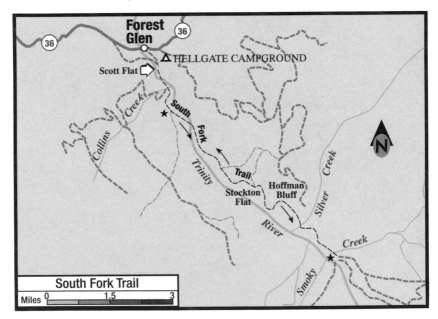

Silver Creek crossing (photo by John Stein)

Points of interest: old-growth forest, old cabin, historic mining road, great sections of single-track riding
Accommodations and services: campground and parking at start of ride; no other services
Supplemental maps or other information: Shasta-Trinity National Forest visitor's map, available from 2400 Washington Street, Redding, CA 96001 (916) 246-5222

GETTING THERE
From Red Bluff (on I-5 in the northwestern corner of California) follow State Highway 36 for 75 miles to Forest Glen. The Hellgate Campground is 0.5 mile to the east. A dirt road will lead you 0.75 mile to the trailhead and parking.

IN THE SADDLE
The trailhead is located amid free campsites at Scott Flat, a sunny meadow surrounded by timber and mountains. Cross the Trinity River on a swinging suspension bridge; watch for salmon and steelhead just arrived from the Pacific.

At the end of the bridge, turn left onto a jeep trail and head upstream along the south bank of the river. Cross Collins Creek (use either the footbridge or the jeep trail). This trail may seem too narrow for vehicles, but be prepared to meet a four-wheel-drive vehicle anyway. There are private lands ahead, and owners use this road for access.

Two miles into the ride climb a steep pitch. The road widens as you briefly enter a logged segment, then again descend to the river. The well-marked trail separates from the river to the left, but you will find it easy to keep on course. The river glides through a parklike setting over a series of gravel bars. Stay on the trail, because the land to either side is posted as private.

At approximately 3 miles, cross a steel bridge, which is as far as vehicles can proceed. As you travel along the north bank, the single track dips and rolls across terraces and seasonal creeks.

Stockton Flat is at approximately the 4-mile point, with a junction to the Cable Creek Trail. (It is a tempting side visit, but it is not a maintained trail.) Climb a steep, 0.4-mile pitch to Hoffman Bluff and earn a great sweeping view in the process. This is a prudent place to walk your bike; in several places, a slip would mean a fast descent to the river.

A quick downhill at the 6-mile point will take you to Silver Creek and another bridge crossing. There is a good place for some wading near the bridge. The trail winds through deep grass and then again enters the forest.

At 7.3 miles, you will arrive at your outbound destination: a dilapidated old cabin and Smoky Creek. Enjoy some poking around, then saddle up and return to the parking area via the same route.

RIDE GUIDE

  0.0 From Scott Flat, ride across swinging bridge, then turn left onto unnamed jeep road.

  0.3 Cross Collins Creek.

  2.1 Climb steep hill.

★ 2.8 Bear left to follow trail.

  2.9 Cross steel bridge.

  3.9 Cross Stockton Flat.

★ 7.3 Smoky Creek. Turn around and retrace route.

 14.6 Scott Flat. End of ride.

Klamath Forest Ride

Submitted by David and Kristina Vandershaf

This road trip combines great river and mountain scenery with lightly traveled roads in one of the more remote regions of California.

Type of ride: road bike
Starting point: Fort Jones
Finishing point: same
Distance: 173 miles
Level of difficulty: moderate
General terrain: mountainous
Traffic conditions: very light
Estimated riding time: 3 days
Best season/time of day to ride: spring through fall
Points of interest: remote northern California countryside, Klamath River
Accommodations and services: campgrounds, several small stores

GETTING THERE

Yreka is approximately 10 miles south of the California-Oregon border on Interstate 5. You may wish to stock up there as there are no stores for the first section of the trip. Two miles south of Yreka, take the State Highway 3 exit west to Fort Jones. The USFS ranger station, at the junction of State Highway 3 and Scott River Road, permits cyclists to park their vehicles in the lot. You can obtain additional information for your ride at this ranger station. Ask the ranger about drinking water availability at the Idlewild Campground (Day 2) if you plan to stay there.

IN THE SADDLE

The elevation at Fort Jones is 2,740 feet; the total elevation gain over this 173-mile tour is 10,800 feet. That should give you a good picture of the type of terrain through which you will be riding. However, there is really only one steep climbing section, so this tour is rated moderate in difficulty.

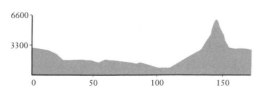

DAY 1

Take Scott River Road in a northwest direction, following the Scott River downstream. At mile 31, switch rivers as you turn left onto State Highway 96 and begin following the Klamath River. Even though this is a major east-west highway, traffic typically remains light, especially on weekdays. Expect some truck traffic.

In Hamburg, you will find your first store on the route. Water and rest rooms are available, making this a good spot for lunch. Seiad Valley, 9 miles farther along the route, also has stores if you want to get in a few more miles of riding before lunch.

Begin your first climb (6 miles) at about mile 50; then lose much of that elevation gain in a quick downhill. At Happy Camp (mile 61), plan to stock up on provisions. This is the last grocery store until day 3 of this tour. The store is 0.1 mile up Indian Creek Road. There are also restaurants, motels, and a ranger station here. If you would like to camp, the Dillon Creek Campground is at mile 83.7. There are no showers available, but there are plenty of swimming holes in both the Klamath River and Dillon Creek.

DAY 2

Continue on State Route 96. At the 100-mile point, you will arrive at an overlook of Ishi Pishi Falls and a store at Somes Bar. No water is available here. Make a left turn onto Salmon River Road and head up the Salmon River for the next 48 miles. The road narrows as you work your way up this narrow canyon; be alert for steep drop-offs on the edges of the right-hand shoulder.

There is another small store at Forks of Salmon at mile 117. Here turn left onto Sawyers Bar Road. The next small, remote town, Sawyers Bar, had a small store that was struggling to remain open as of this writing, but do not count on it for supplies. Five miles past Sawyers Bar is a USFS campground, Idlewild.

DAY 3

To this point in the tour, you have pretty much lost as much altitude as you have gained. The elevation at the starting point on Scott River Road was 2,740 feet; at Idlewild Campground it is 2,540 feet. But now as the road leaves the river begin a steady, steep ascent. Do not schedule this portion of the ride for a hot afternoon! Just for fun, we selected a random section—between miles 144 and 146—in which to measure the average gradient, and we came up with 10.5 percent.

The steepness is maintained all the way to Salmon Mountain Summit, at mile 148 and an elevation of 5,900 feet. This is the high point of the trip. You will see snow-capped mountains nearby in the spring, but the road is kept open year-round, so do not worry about snow closures. Be ready for any type of weather; on one May trip, the temperature was only 42 degrees Fahrenheit on the summit, with a stiff windchill factor as well.

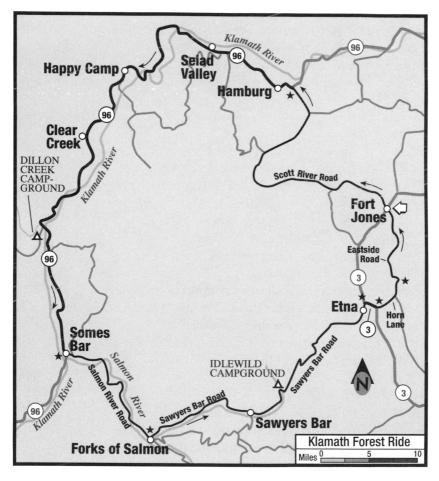

As a reward for all of that climbing, you get a nice long downhill with an approximately 7 percent grade. Watch out for loose rocks—it takes a while for them to work off the road surface because the traffic is so light.

At mile 158, with the elevation back down to 2,880 feet, you will come to the town of Etna. Turn left onto Main Street and treat yourself to a restaurant meal.

You can choose the low-traffic (main) route with some gravel for the return to Fort Jones or take pavement with some traffic on State Highway 3. If you want to follow the main route, turn right (southeast) onto State Highway 3 as you leave Etna. Turn left onto Horn Lane and then left again onto the gravel Eastside Road. After mile 162.5, Eastside Road is paved. Follow it back to Fort Jones at mile 173. For the paved alternate, take Middle Scott Valley Road north out of Etna. State Highway 3 will also take you back to Fort Jones, but it features higher traffic levels.

RIDE GUIDE

    0.0 From ranger station at junction of SR 3 and Scott River Road, ride north on Scott River Road.

★ 31.8 Turn left onto SR 96.

    33.1 Hamburg.

    42.1 Seiad Valley.

    61.0 Happy Camp.

    83.7 Dillon Creek Campground.

    99.6 Somes Bar.

★ 99.9 Turn left onto Salmon River Road.

  117.4 Forks of Salmon.

★ 117.5 Turn left onto Sawyers Bar Road.

  132.7 Sawyers Bar.

  138.2 Idlewild Campground.

  148   Salmon Mountain Summit.

★ 157.8 Etna. Turn left onto Main Street.

★ 158.3 Turn right onto SR 3.

★ 159.7 Turn left onto Horn Lane.

★ 161.1 Turn left onto Eastside Road.

  172.9 Fort Jones. End of ride.

Slammin' Salmon Tour
Submitted by Daniel L. Cikuth

Here is a strenuous 5-day tour that combines both road touring (70 percent) and mountain biking (30 percent) and takes you through some of the most remote regions of northwest California. The tour is capped by a ride through the towering redwoods of Jedediah Smith Redwoods State Park.

Type of ride: road bike
Starting point: Redding
Finishing point: Crescent City
Distance: 228.5 miles
Level of difficulty: hard
General terrain: mountainous
Traffic conditions: light
Estimated riding time: 5 days
Best season/time of day to ride: May to September
Points of interest: old lumbering towns, remote northern California landscape
Accommodations and services: few; see text
Supplemental maps or other information: topo maps, especially of the Siskiyou area, available from Alpine outfitters, 950 Hilltop Drive, Redding, CA (916) 221-7333

GETTING THERE
Redding is 160 miles north of Sacramento on Interstate 5. This is a city of 80,000 people, and it offers numerous bike shops, hotels, and restaurants.

IN THE SADDLE
This tour features the transition from California's northern central valley to the north coastal region. Much of the terrain is mountainous and remote, so it is wise to be prepared for all types of weather. Your bicycle should be in top condition. Use either a mountain bike fitted with road rims and tires or a road touring bike fitted with heavier rims and tires. This may be the perfect tour for using one of the newer "combi" bikes.

The tour is divided into five days, with an average of 50 miles each day. Do not let the low mileages fool you: Several of the days involve some strenuous riding.

Careful planning regarding food and water is important; carry a water filter as potable water resources are scarce on several sections of the tour.

DAY 1

Leave Redding heading west on State Highway 299 (Eureka Way in Redding) toward Whiskeytown Lake. Ten miles of riding will take you to Old Shasta, which served as the county seat in the late 1800s. Another 3 miles takes you to Whiskeytown Lake, part of the Whiskeytown-Shasta-Trinity National Recreation Area.

About 5 miles past the lake, turn north (right) onto Trinity Mountain Road and head toward the old mining town of French Gulch. This is a good town in which to fill all of your water bottles, because water will be scarce for the next 40 miles.

French Gulch also marks the beginning of your first serious stretch of climbing, as signs of civilization begin to fade away. At approximately 12.5 miles north of French Gulch, cross County Line Road. Continue climbing as the paved road turns to gravel. You will get a well-deserved downhill after another 8 miles of climbing, just as you pass near Blue Mountain (elevation 5,336 feet).

In another dozen miles, the route crosses the east fork of the Trinity River. This is a good place to filter some water and enjoy a swim. The road becomes paved for the remainder of the ride to Coffee Creek. Continue northwest on Trinity Mountain Road until the junction with State Highway 3. Turn right (north) onto Highway 3 and you will be at Coffee Creek (which has a small store) in approximately 3 miles. Two miles north of Coffee Creek there is a campsite just off Highway 3 along the main branch of the Trinity River.

DAY 2

Continue on State Highway 3 north towards the small town of Callahan, riding along the Trinity River on a gradual climb of 10 to 12 miles. Then begin a steeper climb to Scott Mountain Pass. Approximately 17 miles north of Coffee Creek, you will reach the 5,401-foot summit of the pass. The Pacific Crest Trail crosses here, and there is a small campground

Taking a break from the climb on Highway 3 (photo by Daniel Cikuth)

(no water) for rest or food preparation. You will probably be in a hurry to enjoy the 10 miles of well-deserved downhill, which takes you into Callahan.

Take the Cecilville Road southwest out of Callahan and get ready for more climbing. The first 10 miles are not very difficult, but the next 5 miles involve rigorous climbing in remote mountainous terrain. As you near the summit, the Pacific Crest Trail will again cross your path. You will be rewarded for your efforts with another 10-mile downhill along the Salmon River into Cecilville. There is a campground about 2 miles before you reach Cecilville and a small store and water supplies in the town itself.

DAY 3

This is probably the least strenuous day on the tour, and it is well-timed because you need to build your strength for day 4. Most of your day will be spent on a gradual downhill following the clear green waters of the south fork of the Salmon River. The scenery is breathtaking, so plan to take your time.

Approximately 18 miles west of Cecilville is a small hamlet called Forks of Salmon. This is where the north and south forks of the Salmon River meet. For the next 17 miles, the river is considered a world-class white-water ride, with many Class 5 rapids. You may get the opportunity to meet some of the men and women who seek to challenge the "Slammin' Salmon."

The Salmon empties into the Klamath River near the town of Somes Bar on State Highway 96. Somes Bar has a small store and water is available there. Members of the Karuk Tribe make their homes along the Klamath here; the Hoop Valley Indian Reservation is situated about 30 miles southwest of Somes Bar.

Turn north onto State Highway 96 along the Klamath for about 20 miles to Dillon Creek Campground on the west side of the highway. There are many nice campsites and potable water in this campground. Get to bed early because Day 4 and the Siskiyou Wilderness await.

DAY 4

The Siskiyou Wilderness is perhaps the most remote wild area in northern California. Most of the day's ride will be off-road, so you should have plenty of food and water with you.

Scenic vista from Trinity Mountain Road (photo by Daniel Cikuth)

From Dillon Creek Campground, backtrack south on State Highway 96 towards Somes Bar for approximately 2 miles until you see a sign on the right for Sidewinder Road. Take a right onto Sidewinder and get ready to climb. They named this road for the rattlesnake that travels sideways in a continuous curving motion, and you will learn why.

You will come to a sign that reads "Eyesee G-O Road 11 miles." (Our cycling computer later put this distance at more like 14 miles.) Continue climbing on Sidewinder Road until you reach USFS Route

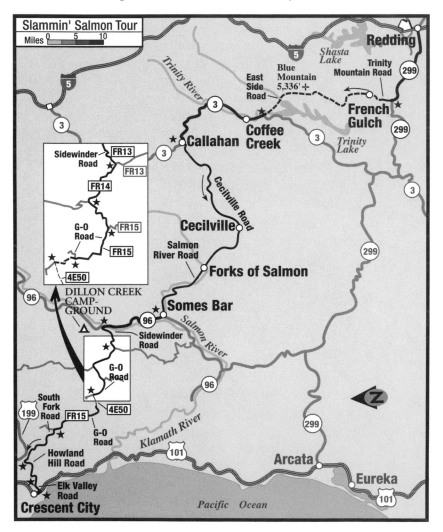

15, which is also called the Gasquet-Orleans (G-O) Road. Take a right onto the Gasquet-Orleans Road and continue until it ends.

Why does the road end? In the 1980s, logging companies wanted to build a highway between the towns of Gasquet (pronounced Gas-kee) and Orleans. The companies hoped to log old-growth pine, cedar, and fir in the Blue Creek watershed. However, the Karuk Tribe went to court and successfully blocked the plan, claiming that the area was a sacred spiritual place where religious rites of passage occurred. (Some of the tribespeople still use this area today for vision quests.) The road you are following is for all intents and purposes a two-lane highway with an 8-mile break of double track in the middle.

Take the gravel road to the left just before the end of the G-O Road and follow it down into Elk Valley. Keep a watch on the left for a trail blocked by boulders. This is Boundary Trail 4E50. The large rock out-cropping on a mountain to the northwest is Chimney Rock.

Turn left onto Boundary Trail 4E50. You will have to do some walking around boulders and fallen trees, but it is not all that difficult to navigate the northern portion of the G-O Road on a bicycle.

Near the end of Boundary Trail 4E50, a mammoth rock formation sits like a sentinel over the Blue Creek watershed. This rock has been nicknamed the "Doctor Rock." It is said that area tribespeople go there to ask the spirits of ancestors for wisdom and instruction. Please behave respectfully in this area that remains important to Native Americans.

Boundary Trail 4E50 ends at the opposite terminus of G-O Road. Follow G-O Road approximately 18 miles to the Big Flat Camp along Hurdygurdy Creek, just past the junction with Big Flat Road.

DAY 5

This is another leisurely riding day, taking you along the south fork of the Smith River and into Crescent City. At Big Flat Camp, G-O Road becomes South Fork Road. This road takes you 10 miles northwest to the small town of Hiouchi (pronounced Hi-oo-chee) and the junction with US Highway 199.

A left turn on State Highway 199 here would take you to Crescent City, but choose instead the Howland Hill Road and enjoy the redwoods of Jedediah Smith Redwoods State Park. Be sure to stop at the Stout Grove, where the tallest trees in this special park are located. When the fog rolls in, the crowns of these lofty giants are lost in the mist far above.

Continue on Howland Hill Road into Crescent City, a bustling coastal town with all the services you will need. Crescent City was established in 1852, a year after a party of gold seekers discovered its harbor. Today it is the seat of Del Norte County and is California's northernmost community of size.

RIDE GUIDE

   0.0 From Redding ride west on SR 299.
   10.2 Old Shasta.

Cyclist at the Scott Mountain summit on Highway 3 (photo by Craig Bunas)

13.3 Whiskeytown Lake.
★ 18.3 Turn right onto Trinity Mountain Road.
35.3 Trinity Summit. Route changes name to East Side Road.
★ 61.3 Turn right onto SR 3.
★ 86.3 Callahan. Turn left onto Cecilville Road.
116.3 Cecilville.
134.3 Forks of Salmon. Route changes name to Salmon River
Road.
★ 151.4 Somes Bar. Turn right onto SR 96.
★ 168.8 Turn left onto Sidewinder Road (FR 13).
★ 176.2 Turn right onto FR 14.
★ 177.3 At Cedar Camp, bear left onto unnamed road.
★ 179.5 Turn right onto G-O Road (FR 15).
★ 182.8 Bear left to continue on FR 15; G-O Road leaves route.
★ 184.9 Look carefully and turn onto Trail 4E50.
192.9 Ride onto G-O Road (FR 15).
209.1 Turn left onto South Fork Road (CR 427).
221.1 Hiouchi. Turn left onto Howland Hill Road.
227.0 Turn left onto Elk Valley Road.
★ 227.9 Turn right onto US 101.
228.5 Crescent City. End of ride.

Whiskeytown Lake Loop

Submitted by Allen Kost

This 2,200-foot climbing ride will take you to some grand views of
Whiskeytown Lake, one of California's prettiest human-made lakes.

Type of ride: mountain bike
Starting point: Whiskeytown Lake Information Center parking lot
Finishing point: same
Distance: 14 miles round-trip
Level of difficulty: moderate
General terrain: climbing on dirt road 7 miles to lookout; 2,200-foot gain
Traffic conditions: light

Estimated riding time: 2.5 to 3.5 hours
Best season/time of day to ride: spring and fall
Points of interest: great views of Whiskeytown Lake and surroundings
Accommodations and services: information center at base of climb
Supplemental maps or other information: detailed information about the Whiskeytown-Shasta-Trinity National Recreation Area available from the Shasta-Trinity National Forest, 2400 Washington Avenue, Redding, CA 96001

GETTING THERE

Redding is 160 miles north of Sacramento on Interstate 5. Follow State Highway 299 for 7 miles west of Redding, passing through Old Shasta State Historic Park 2 miles before reaching the parking lot at the Whiskeytown Lake Information Center.

IN THE SADDLE

The route that will take you on this 2,200-foot climb to the South Fork Mountain Lookout begins directly across State Highway 299 from the Whiskeytown Lake Information Center. Turn off the dirt road to the left almost immediately and pass through a metal gate. Start your 7-mile climb up the hill.

As you near the top of the climb, take the left fork in the road to reach the lookout. You may see hang gliders or parasailers launching from a rock ramp near the top. You will get some fantastic views of Whiskeytown Lake.

Established in 1965 as part of the Federal Bureau of Reclamation's Central Valley Project, the Whiskeytown-Shasta-Trinity National Recreation Area consists of three units: Whiskeytown Lake, Shasta Lake, and Clair Engle (Trinity) Lake. Below the Whiskeytown Dam, Clear Creek winds through steep gorges and rocky hills. This was once a major gold-and silver-producing stream.

After soaking up enough views, return to the parking lot by following the same road you climbed. Watch your speed on the dirt road. You may encounter

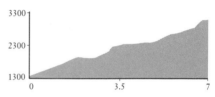

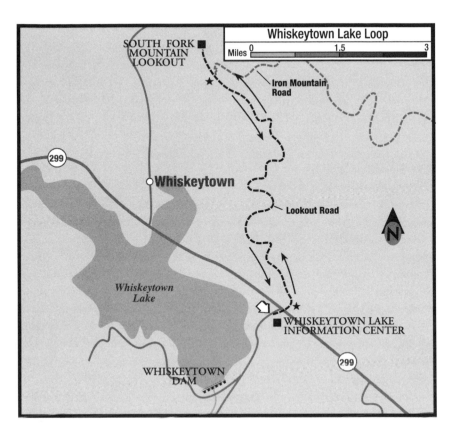

a car or two, but for the most part, you should have the road to yourself.

Once back at the Information Center, take the short trail from the parking lot down to the lake for a refreshing dip in the cool, clear water. Directions for other rides in the area can be obtained at the Information Center.

RIDE GUIDE

    0.0 From parking lot, ride across SR 299 onto Lookout Road.

★   0.1 Turn left and ride through metal gate.

★   6.3 Take left fork in road.

    7.0 South Fork Mountain Lookout. Turn around and return same way you came.

  14.0 End of ride.

Avenue of the Giants
Submitted by Stan Hansen

This world-famous scenic road meanders peacefully through a living museum of 43,000 acres that contains the world's tallest trees: the California redwoods. The bicycle is the perfect vehicle from which to view these magnificent trees.

Type of ride: road bike
Starting point: Pepperwood
Finishing point: Phillipsville (or back to Pepperwood)
Distance: 31 miles (62 round-trip)
Level of difficulty: easy
General terrain: flat to rolling with a few easy grades
Traffic conditions: light during the week; heavy on spring through fall
   weekends
Estimated riding time: 3 to 4 hours with lots of looking
Best season/time of day to ride: July to October
Points of interest: the redwoods of Humboldt County
Accommodations and services: small stores, restaurants en route;
   campgrounds
Supplemental maps or other information: AAA Northwestern California map

GETTING THERE
From the coastal town of Eureka, in the far northwest corner of California, turn south onto US Highway 101 for 30 miles to the Pepperwood/ Avenue of the Giants exit. There is shoulder parking available. Or turn off Highway 101 in Scotia (25 miles south of Eureka) and start from this quaint, company-owned logging town. This option will add 5 miles of pedaling to your tour.

IN THE SADDLE
You can ride the Avenue of the Giants (signed in some locations as State Highway 254) as either a

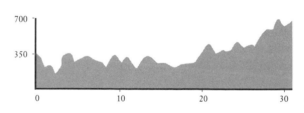

one-way 31-mile tour or as an out-and-back ride of 62 miles. If you have the time for the round trip, the forest and the lighting conditions will almost guarantee a different riding experience in each direction. The road is generally not heavily trafficked, and the elevation gain along the

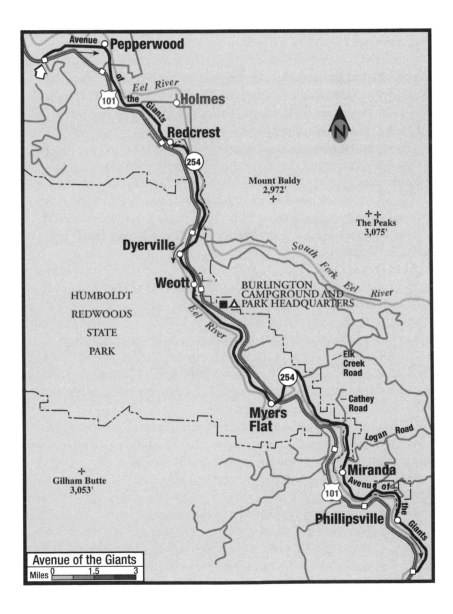

entire route is only about 300 feet, with lots of rolling and some flat terrain.

Note: You will be riding in and out of sun-dappled roadway for the majority of this tour and you may not be easily noticed. While the route usually carries only light traffic, make yourself noticeable by wearing light clothing, wearing a helmet, and using a "fanny bumper" (a tied-on orange safety triangle), with fluorescent edging if available.

The town of Pepperwood sits among some nice redwood groves next to the Eel River, which serenely parallels the entire Avenue of the Giants route. The road gradually climbs to the outskirts of Holmes and Redcrest. Watch for the Drury-Chaney Grove. There is a 2-mile hike through primeval forest that is well worth the walk.

At about 8 miles, you will enter the outer edge of Humboldt Redwoods State Park and get a nice 2-mile downhill run through more redwood forest. Keep your speed down so as not to miss any sights.

At 11 miles, an exit takes you across Highway 101 to the town of Dyerville, with major services. Shortly thereafter, you will see a turnoff for the Dyerville Giant. This tree was 1,600 years old when it fell; scientists have dated it to A.D. 491.

Leaving the Dyerville area, remain on the Avenue of the Giants and cross over Highway 101 to continue south on the west side of the highway, still paralleling the Eel River. Pass the hiker/biker camp for the Humboldt Redwoods State Park and, just past the small town of Weott, enter some of the most spectacular stands of redwood giants in the park.

At 14 miles, you will reach the Burlington Campground and Park Headquarters. This mostly flat stretch continues to provide great views of the forest from almost every angle. (This is where a car ride just does not cut it.)

In another 4 miles, you will reach Myers Flat, with a few store fronts, restaurants, and antique stores. Just past Myers Flat, the Avenue crosses under Highway 101 and follows its east side. The road begins a steeper—though not difficult—climb and then peaks and descends gradually through several dense groves for the next couple of miles. At 21 miles, you will pass the junction with Elk Creek Road.

At the 24-mile point, after the Cathey Road junction, the redwoods begin to dwindle and you can begin to see some of the open valley area of the state park. A challenging short grade takes you into Miranda

Taking a break with one of the giants (photo by Stan Hansen)

where there are a couple of cafes and small stores for stocking up on supplies.

At 27 miles, ride through the last few groves associated with the Avenue of the Giants. Pass through the town of Phillipsville where you can either meet your shuttle car or turn around to enjoy the road from another vantage point. The Avenue of the Giants merges with Highway 101 at the 31-mile point. There are more campgrounds farther to the south, including Richardson's Grove State Park and Standish-Hickey State Park. There is also a popular youth hostel in Leggett.

RIDE GUIDE

  0.0 From Pepperwood exit on US 101, ride east on Avenue of the Giants (SR 254).
  0.8 Avenue of the Giants road markers.
  2.2 Pepperwood.
  7.5 Humboldt Redwoods State Park.
  11.7 Dyerville Giant turnoff.
  14.2 Burlington Campground and Park Headquarters.
  18.8 Myers Flat.
  21.0 Elk Creek Road junction.
  23.6 Cathey Road junction.
  25.4 Miranda.
  29.2 Phillipsville.
  31.0 US 101. End of ride.

Redding to Ferndale
Submitted by Allen Kost

This 2- to 3-day road tour will take you from the northern Sacramento Valley over and through the Coast Range to the Victorian town of Ferndale.

Type of ride: road bike
Starting point: Redding
Finishing point: Ferndale
Distance: 150 miles

Level of difficulty: difficult (especially as a 2-day tour)
General terrain: some steep climbs in mountainous terrain
Traffic conditions: light traffic on mostly two-lane roads with no shoulders
Estimated riding time: 2 to 3 days
Best season/time of day to ride: May, June, September, October
Points of interest: beautiful, varied scenery; Victorian town of Ferndale
Accommodations and services: all services in Redding and Ferndale; few services in smaller towns along the way
Supplemental maps or other information: northwestern California AAA map, a good backup

The three Shastas: dam, mountain, and lake (photo by Alan Kost)

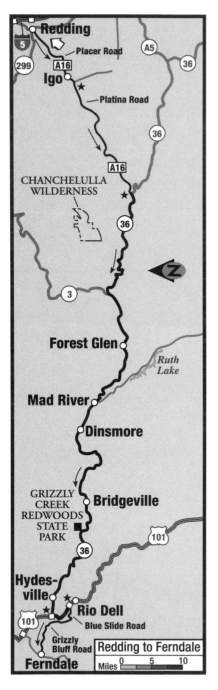

GETTING THERE

The ride starts in downtown Redding, which is located approximately 160 miles north of Sacramento on Interstate 5.

IN THE SADDLE

Starting in Redding, head west on Placer Road (A16) for 12 miles to Igo. Turn left at the stop sign in Igo to stay on Placer Road. One more mile brings you to the junction of Placer Road, Clear Creek Road to the left, Gas Point Road straight ahead, and Platina Road to the right. Turn right onto Platina Road. In the next 12 miles, you will pass the Ono Store and a fire station.

At the junction with State Highway 36, turn right onto the highway toward the Platina Store. You are approximately 40 miles into the ride and you will be entering the mountains that separate the Sacramento Valley from the Pacific Ocean. Be sure you have enough food and water for the ride. The small stores you will pass along the way are not always well-stocked and may not be open.

Approximately 5 miles after turning onto Highway 36, pass a ranger station and then undertake a 3-mile climb up Goods Mountain (the summit is at 3,810 feet).

From the summit it is nearly 12 miles to the junction with State

Highway 3. Pass Wild-
wood Road on the right
and USFS Route 30
(Wild Mad Road) on the
left. Remain on State

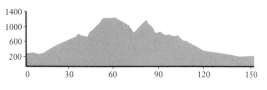

Highway 36 (State Highway 3 ends at this junction) and follow it 10 miles into Forest Glen. This town is a reliable source for food and water. There are also two forest service campgrounds 1 and 2 miles before Forest Glen, your best bets for an overnight stop.

Continue on State Highway 36 and just past Forest Glen start a 7-mile climb to the top of South Fork Summit (elevation 4,090 feet). This is the longest climb and the highest point of the trip. The 7 miles after the summit give you a downhill run to the town of Mad River. In another 7 miles, arrive at Dinsmore, where there is a guest lodge. Continue on State Highway 36 for nearly 18 miles to Bridgeville, which—as its name suggests—has a bridge. Food and water are available here.

You will now be entering the redwoods area. The Grizzly Creek Redwoods State Park is 7 miles beyond Bridgeville. This is a state campground nestled in a redwood forest where Grizzly Creek enters the Van Duzen River. You can enjoy a hot shower and some great campsites.

From Grizzly Creek, State Highway 36 follows the Van Duzen River to Carlotta and then climbs to Hydesville. Turn left at Hydesville, remaining on State Highway 36 for 3 more miles until its end at US Highway 101.

Turn left onto US Highway 101 and follow it for approximately 5 miles south to the Blue Slide Road exit at the north end of Rio Dell. Turn right onto Blue Slide Road, and follow it west and then north where it becomes Grizzly Bluff Road. Follow Grizzly Bluff Road for 11 miles into the Victorian town of Ferndale.

In Ferndale, you will find some of the finest examples of Victorian architecture north of San Francisco. First settled in 1863 by Danish immigrants, the historic town was partially leveled by a 1992 earthquake that registered 6.9 on the Richter scale. Architecture lovers can take a walking tour and obtain a free guide to the historic buildings at the Chamber of Commerce (248 Francis).

For a 2-day camping trip, camp the first night 1 to 2 miles east of Forest Glen. For a 3-day camping trip, spend the first night at a forest service campground (water only) near Platina: 5 miles west of Platina, turn left onto FR28N10 and travel 1.7 miles on an unpaved road to the campground.

RIDE GUIDE

    0.0 From Redding, ride west on Placer Road (County Road A16).

    12.0 Igo. At stop sign, turn left to stay on Placer Road.

★ 13.0 Turn right onto Platina Road (County Road A16).

★ 39.5 Turn right onto SR 36.

    60.3 Junction with SR 3. Continue on SR 36.

    70.4 Forest Glen.

    85.3 Mad River.

    92.0 Dinsmore.

    109.5 Bridgeville.

    116.4 Grizzly Creek Redwoods State Park.

    130.4 Hydesville.

★133.4 Turn left onto US 101.

★138.4 Turn right onto Blue Slide Road.

    142.4 Ride straight onto Grizzly Bluff Road.

    148.9 Ferndale.

Region 2
Wine Country

A cool spot among the vineyards (photo by Alan Bloom)

The Unknown Coast

Submitted by Jill McIntyre

This ride begins and ends in Humboldt County, well known for its groves of Redwoods. You will also visit the only section of California coastline that is not served by a major highway; it is nicknamed the Unknown Coast.

Type of ride: road bike
Starting point: Eureka
Finishing point: same
Distance: 145 miles
Level of difficulty: moderate
General terrain: rolling hills with several steeper climbs
Traffic conditions: light except in Highway 101 corridor
Estimated riding time: 5 days
Best season/time of day to ride: August, September
Points of interest: Carson Mansion, Ferndale, redwoods
Accommodations and services: all services available along the route
Supplemental maps or other information: AAA Northwestern California map

GETTING THERE

Eureka is on US Highway 101, approximately a 6-hour drive north of San Francisco. The Carson Mansion, at the corner of 2nd and M Streets, is Eureka's most visited site, built by a lumber magnate next to his sprawling mills. Since the jagged roofline of the Carson Mansion is visible from nearly every quarter of the city, the route begins and ends here.

IN THE SADDLE

This loop is designed as a leisurely 5-day road biking tour through Humboldt County in northern California. (You can double up the mileages on several days to provide a 3- or 4-day ride as well.) The route begins and ends in Eureka, the largest California city on the

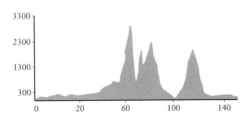

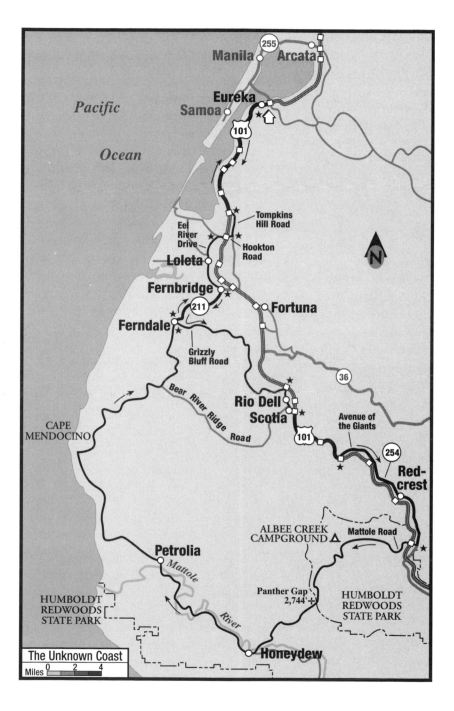

north coast. Along the way, you will see well-preserved Victorian architecture and some of the planet's most awe-inspiring trees: the redwoods.

DAY 1

Eureka, as one might expect, owes its name to the town's founder, James Ryan, who shouted the Greek for "I have found it" as he drove his boat onto the mudflats of Humboldt Bay in 1850. Ryan proceeded to survey and plat the town's first lots in the same year. Eureka quickly prospered around the dual economies of redwood lumbering and shipping throughout Humboldt Bay's narrow channel.

Leave Eureka on Highway 101 and wind through the pastures of the dairy country along the Eel River. This river was named by the Gregg Party, a government-financed 1849 expedition comprised of traders and explorers who were charged with further opening the California interior. The expedition happened upon a small number of Indians laden with freshwater eels captured in the river, and the river was named accordingly.

At 15 miles, enter Loleta, which was originally named Swauger after an early settler but was renamed when the town became a shipping point for the surrounding dairy region. The town's current name suggests some of the Portuguese influence of the early immigrants who arrived as milkers on the dairy farms and slowly established herds of their own. Today, dairy products account for nearly half of Humboldt County's agricultural income. The Loleta Cheese Factory offers tours and a tasting room where you can sample some of the cheeses produced in the area. Another 5 miles will bring you to the Fernbridge, a seven-arch structure designed with a nod to Roman architecture. There is camping at the Humboldt County Fairgrounds in Ferndale.

DAY 2

As you continue, the rich pasturelands of the dairy country begin to give way to the towering redwood forests. Ferndale, situated on the wide delta plain of the Eel River, was first established by Danish immigrants in 1864. Victorian architecture enthusiasts will love Ferndale. Just about every building on Main Street exemplifies this period.

Before entering the Avenue of the Giants and the Humboldt Redwoods State Park, cycle through the lumber towns of Rio Dell and Scotia; the loggers and millworkers at the huge Pacific Lumber

Rolling along on the Avenue of the Giants (photo by Marianne Tamm)

Company mill established in 1886 came largely from Nova Scotia. The mill covers some 400 acres. Scotia now bills itself as one of the country's last company-owned towns, once a common phenomenon in the logging and mining industry. You can visit the logging museum and take a self-guided tour of the mill. You can still see the effects of the devastating earthquake-caused fire in 1992 that destroyed Scotia's entire downtown business district.

This company town that lumber built stands in stark contrast to the redwood forests through which you will be riding in just a few miles; you owe yourself the opportunity to take some time in Scotia to better understand the industry intended to help build a nation hungry for wood products.

Today, approximately 95 percent of the original California redwood groves have been logged. Although they are fast-growing trees, it will take hundreds of years to replace the giant trees that have been all but logged out. The movement to protect these ancient trees—some are 2,000 years or older—began in the mid-1800s with the establishment of the Mariposa Grove in Yosemite National Park. The first groves in

One of the many hiker-biker camps in Northern California (photo by Marianne Tamm)

northern California were set aside in 1921 in an effort spearheaded by the Save-the-Redwoods League. In part, the league's mission was to "rescue from destruction representative areas of our primeval forests." Self-guiding maps with much more history about the redwoods are available at the entrance to Humboldt Redwoods State Park and the Avenue of the Giants. (See Ride 5 for more information about this section of the tour.) A visitor center at the Humboldt Redwoods main campground offers films and other presentations. Allow time for gawking and photos. Make sure to bring along a wide-angle lens—remember, these rank as the world's tallest living beings, and many of these trees are 350 feet tall or taller.

A 36-mile day will take you to Albee Creek Campground.

DAY 3

After drifting through the green tunnels of the Redwoods, turn again toward the coast, following the winding Mattole Road through Honeydew and Petrolia on the return trip to Ferndale. Along with Ferndale and Scotia, Petrolia and Honeydew were badly damaged by the 1992 earthquake (rated at 6.9 on the Richter scale). The services are sparse in this section, so plan to bring along some extra food and water just in case.

Camping is available at AW Way County Park, 5 miles beyond the Honeydew Store.

DAY 4

This area of California is called the Unknown Coast because it is the only section of the coast in the state that has no major highway running alongside it. It can represent a challenging ride for cyclists who do not handle hills well. For the person really looking for rugged riding, there are a few unpaved hilly sections as well. The rewards? Isolated mountains, valleys, and beaches with few other visitors and little traffic. Most of the cars will stick to US Highway 101 and bypass the Unknown Coast. You will have the fun of reaching near Cape Mendocino, the westernmost point in the lower forty-eight states.

DAY 5

This is the return leg through a now-familiar area between Ferndale and Eureka. The Ride Guide will take you back to the US Highway 101 corridor and the Carson Mansion in Eureka.

RIDE GUIDE

 0.0 From the Carson Mansion, turn left onto 2nd Street.

 0.8 At т, turn right onto Commercial and then left onto Waterfront Street.

 1.6 Turn right onto Koster Street.

★ 2.1 Turn left onto Wabash and then right onto Broadway (US 101).

★ 8.6 Turn right onto Tompkins Hill Road.

★ 11.7 Turn right onto Hookton Road and then ride straight onto Eel River Drive.

 14.7 Loleta.

 16.7 Bear right to continue on Eel River Drive toward Fernbridge.

★ 17.2 Turn right onto SR 211 toward Ferndale.

 21.2 Ferndale. Turn right onto Van Ness.

 21.7 Turn left onto 5th Street.

 22.3 Turn left onto Shaw Street.

 22.5 Turn right onto Main Street.

★ 22.7 Turn left onto Ocean Street, which becomes Grizzly Bluff Road.

★ 35.3 Turn right onto Wildwood Avenue. Rio Dell.

 36.3 Cross bridge and continue into Scotia. Route becomes Main Street.

★ 37.8 Turn left onto US 101 South.

★ 42.5 Exit onto the Avenue of the Giants.

 49.7 Redcrest.

★ 53.8 Turn right onto Mattole Road toward Honeydew.

 59.0 Albee Creek Campground.

 68.6 Panther Gap summit.

 76.8 Cross one-lane bridge and turn right toward Honeydew store.

 82.1 Gravel stretch for 0.2 mile.

 88.6 Gravel stretch for 1 mile.

 92.0 Petrolia store.

 92.5 Gravel stretch for 0.8 mile.

 97.5 Public access to beach.

112.4 First summit of Bear River Ridge.

★ 122.4 Ferndale. Turn right onto Ocean and then left onto 5th Street.

123.1 Humboldt County Fairgrounds.

123.6 Turn left onto Main Street/Fernbridge Road toward Fernbridge.

★ 127.6 After bridge, turn left at intersection.

128.1 Turn left onto Eel River Drive.

130.1 Loleta.

★ 132.7 At US 101, follow overpass and then turn left onto Hookton Road.

★ 133.1 Turn left onto Tompkins Hill Road.

136.2 Continue straight onto US 101 North.

142.7 Turn left onto Wabash and then turn right onto Koster.

143.2 Turn left onto Waterfront.

144.0 Turn right onto Commercial and then left onto 2nd Street.

144.8 Carson Mansion. End of ride.

Vineyard Loop
Submitted by Alan Bloom

This easy loop ride will take you past at least a dozen wineries. If you are not into sampling the grape, the ride still offers many scenic vistas of this heartland of California's vineyard country.

Type of ride: road bike
Starting point: Healdsburg
Finishing point: same
Distance: 33 miles
Level of difficulty: easy
General terrain: flat to moderate rolling hills
Traffic conditions: light traffic (a little heavier on weekends) on two-lane roads with narrow shoulders
Estimated riding time: 2 hours, plus any time spent wine tasting
Best season/time of day to ride: spring, after the rains
Points of interest: at least a dozen wineries right along the route

Accommodations and services: all services in Healdsburg; camping in nearby Asti

Supplemental maps or other information: Krebs North San Francisco Bay/Sacramento map, available in many area bicycle shops

GETTING THERE

From San Francisco, take US Highway 101 north over the Golden Gate Bridge, past Santa Rosa to Healdsburg. Take the downtown Healdsburg Avenue exit and continue to Matheson Street. Turn left into the municipal parking lot.

IN THE SADDLE

This is a fairly easy loop ride, beginning and ending in Healdsburg, rated for families, novices, or hardier riders with a taste for wine. The Vineyard Loop ride features more wineries per mile than probably any other single bike ride. If you want to learn about, sample, or just smell wines, this is the ride for you.

There are many outstanding wineries along the Vineyard Loop. (photo by Alan Bloom)

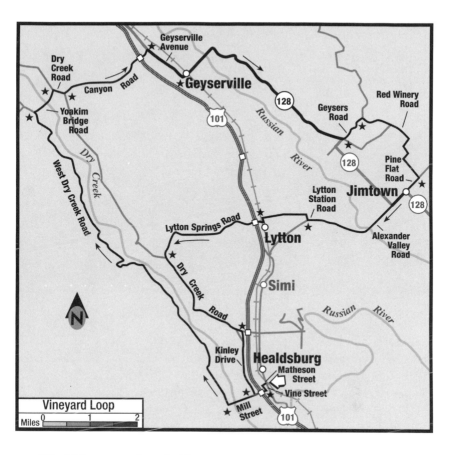

Healdsburg was founded by Harmon Heald, an erstwhile miner who found no luck in the gold fields. Heald built a cabin and lean-to that gradually grew into a general store and post office. In 1856, he purchased a large tract of land at a public auction at the price of $2 per acre. The community that grew around this large plaza went under several names, including Sotoyome, Heald's Store, Stringtown, and Russian River. It became Healdsburg when Heald filed his subdivision plan in 1857.

You will be cycling through the Dry Creek and Alexander Valley wine-growing regions, passing more than a dozen wineries along the way. Many of the wineries have bicycle racks because so many of their customers arrive on two wheels. Just remember to not overdo the tasting—it is a 32-mile bicycle ride.

At the 10-mile point, turn right off West Dry Creek Road onto

Downtown Geyserville (photo by Alan Bloom)

Yoakim Bridge Road. If you then turn left onto Dry Creek Road at 10.5 miles, you will come to Warm Springs Dam in about 5 miles. Here there is camping, boating, swimming, fishing, and a visitor's center at the dam. However, the main route turns right at Dry Creek Road and then left onto Canyon Road.

At the 13-mile point, cross under the freeway and ride into Geyserville. This town is named for geothermal fields located just off State Highway 128, which you will follow out of Geyserville. In 1847, while chasing a bear, Bill Elliott, a Cloverdale resident, stumbled upon what are today called The Geysers. Elliott hurried home with the news that he had found "the gates of Hades themselves." They were later developed by a couple of entrepreneurs into California's first spa. The Geysers were later the site of the world's largest geothermal electric power plant complex, and they played host to hundreds of scientists in the United Nations Symposium on the Development and Utilization of Geothermal Energy. It is a long and strenuous climb up to the geothermal fields, but this ride avoids that climb by turning onto Geysers Road, immediately followed by a turn onto Red Winery Road at about the 19-mile point.

Pine Flat Road becomes State Highway 128, taking you into Jimtown, where there is a neat little "old-timey" store that is a favorite refueling stop for local cyclists.

As you leave Jimtown, State Highway 128 changes to Alexander Valley Road. Watch carefully for the right-hand turn off Alexander Valley Road onto Lytton Station Road, as there is no good landmark. It occurs at about 24.5 miles, right after a sweeping turn to the left, 2.1 miles beyond Jimtown. Lytton Station Road makes a sharp left-hand turn just before the freeway, and then you turn right over the railroad tracks onto Lytton Springs Road at about 26 miles.

After passing the Healdsburg Airport on your left, turn left on Dry Creek Road at mile 28.6 and head back toward Healdsburg. See the Ride Guide for directions into Healdsburg and back to the municipal parking lot on Matheson Street.

RIDE GUIDE

0.0 From Matheson Street parking lot in Healdsburg, turn right and then immediately left onto Vine Street.

★ 0.2 Turn right onto Mill Street, which becomes Westside Road after passing under US 101.

★ 1.1 Turn right onto West Dry Creek Road.

★ 9.9 Turn right onto Yoakim Bridge Road.

★ 10.5 Turn right onto Dry Creek Road.

★ 10.8 Turn left onto Canyon Road.

★ 13.0 Turn right onto Geyserville Avenue (SR 128).

★ 14.0 Geyserville. Turn left to follow SR 128.

★ 18.6 Turn left onto Geysers Road.

★ 19.2 Turn right onto Red Winery Road.

★ 21.6 Turn right onto Pine Flat Road.

★ 24.6 Turn right onto Lytton Station Road.

★ 25.9 Lytton. Turn right to continue on Lytton Springs Road.

★ 28.6 Turn left onto Dry Creek Road.

★ 31.1 Turn right onto Kinley Drive.

32.5 Turn left onto Mill Street/Westside Road.

32.7 Turn left onto Vine Street and then right onto Matheson Street.

32.9 Matheson Street parking lot. End of ride.

Clear Lake to the Coast
Submitted by Bob Wall

The coastal mountain range and Pacific vistas, ancient redwood forests, and vineyards are strung like pearls along this 176-mile, 3-day tour.

Type of ride: road bike
Starting point: Lakeport
Finishing point: same
Distance: 176 miles
Level of difficulty: moderate (multiday tour)
General terrain: gently to moderately rolling; some steeper climbs in the coastal range
Traffic conditions: light traffic on two-lane roads
Estimated riding time: 3 days
Best season/time of day to ride: spring through fall
Points of interest: Navarro River Redwoods State Park, Pacific coast views, Fort Bragg historic logging town, "Cabot Cove" (Mendocino)
Accommodations and services: all services and camping available along the route
Supplemental maps or other information: AAA Northwestern California map

GETTING THERE
This tour begins and ends in Lakeport, just off State Highway 20, between Interstate 5 and US Highway 101, approximately 125 miles north of San Francisco. Lakeport sits on the western shore of Clear Lake. The route directions begin on 11th Street in Lakeport.

IN THE SADDLE

DAY 1
Follow 11th Street west out of Lakeport; it becomes Scotts Valley Road. At the junction with State Highway 20 near Lower Blue Lake, turn left onto State Highway 20 and continue north past Lower and Upper Blue Lakes. The road remains flat with only one short hill as you climb into the next valley. Pass the J-S Ranch at mile 20 in the ride; you can often see buffalo grazing in the pastures here.

At mile 24, you can take a 0.25-mile side trip to the left on Inlet Road for a quick swim in Lake Mendocino.

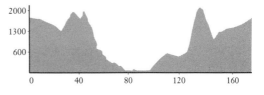

At mile 25, turn right at the Redwood Valley turnoff, go left at the Boulevard and a stop. Continue 0.8 mile to the next boulevard and stop and turn right for 0.2 mile. Turn right again at the next boulevard. Now continue north on North State Street.

Ride along next to US Highway 101 to mile 28, where you will begin the long, easy ascent to Ridgewood Pass at mile 35. This is the highest point (1,953 feet) that US Highway 101 reaches in California.

From Ridgewood Pass, it is a nice downhill into Willits, the home of the Skunk Train, an old logging train that takes you through the redwoods to Fort Bragg on the coast. Watch for your turn to the left on State Highway 20 at the first stoplight. In 2 miles you will come to a KOA, which makes a good overnight stop.

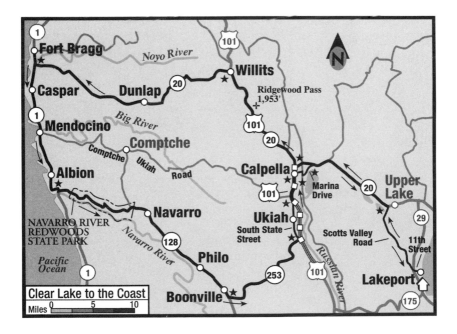

DAY 2

Plan to stock up on food and water in Willits, for there are no services for the next 32 miles. Leave the Willits area on State Highway 20 and climb and descend rolling hills through the pine and redwood forests along a two-lane road heading west toward the Pacific. At Dunlap (approximately mile 55), there are no services other than bathrooms and a picnic area.

Twenty miles after Dunlap, State Highway 20 joins US Highway 1. Take a quick side trip to the historic logging town of Fort Bragg, pausing on the bridge to look at the picturesque fishing town of Noyo. Then turn south down US Highway 1 and tour through the towns of Caspar and Pine Grove.

You may very well recognize Mendocino as the fictional Cabot Cove in the popular television series "Murder She Wrote." There is a definite East Coast fishing village feel to the town, known locally as a haven for artists and craftspeople. Van Damme State Park is just 2.5 miles to the south at mile 88.

DAY 3

Continue on Highway 1 past Little River and on to Albion (a small store just after the bridge) and then to the Navarro River. Do not cross the river, but turn left onto State Highway 128 and follow the north bank of the Navarro. You will pass through large groves of ancient redwoods as you ride in the Navarro River Redwoods State Park. There is a grocery store in the small town of Navarro.

In the next 9 miles between Navarro and Philo, you will pass seven wineries. If you have a penchant for tasting rooms, keep in mind that there are still a few miles to go. However, you will also pass Hendy Woods State Park, which has campsites available.

Just after Philo, pass the small Indian Creek County Park. This campground among the redwoods has a great swimming hole and is one of northern California's best-kept secrets.

Continue on State Highway 128 south to Boonville. If you are not a wine fan, Boonville has a nice microbrewery. It is also the home of "Boontling," a local dialect used here for many years (see Ride 12). Load up on food and water, because you have another 30-mile segment without services coming up.

Less than 2 miles south of Boonville, turn left onto State Highway

253. There is a long uphill to a flat summit that follows a ridge. From here you will get some great views of the surrounding countryside. Then drop down into Ukiah and rejoin the US Highway 101 corridor. Turn left onto State Street, which will take you into downtown Ukiah (with a population of about 10,000, the largest town along this route).

Remain on State Street as you head north until you come to the four-way stop in Calpella. Turn right onto Moore Street for 0.2 miles, right onto Calpella Drive/East Side Road for 0.1 mile, then left onto Marina Drive. You will pass Lake Mendocino, which has a nice campground if you have had enough riding for the day.

It is still 24 miles down State Highway 20 and Scotts Valley Road back to the town of Lakeport.

RIDE GUIDE

    0.0 From Lakeport, ride west on 11th Street.

    0.8 Route becomes Scotts Valley Road.

★ 12.0 At the ⊤, turn left onto SR 20.

★ 25.0 Calpella. Turn right onto North State Street.

  25.8 Turn right onto US 101 (SR 20).

  27.0 Redwood Valley Cellars.

★ 41.0 Willits. Turn left onto SR 20.

  55.2 Dunlap.

★ 75.3 Turn right onto SR 1.

  77.0 Fort Bragg. Turn around and ride south on SR 1.

  81.3 Caspar.

  85.5 Mendocino.

  93.4 Albion.

★ 96.2 Turn left onto SR 128.

 108.1 Navarro.

 116.7 Indian Creek County Park.

 121.2 Philo.

★126.3 Turn left onto SR 253.

 145.3 Turn left onto South State Street.

★147.3 Turn left onto US 101.

 150.1 Calpella.

 150.9 Turn right onto Moore Street.

 151.1 Turn right onto Calpella Drive (East Side Road).

151.2 Turn left onto Marina Drive.

152.6 Ride onto SR 20.

★ 164.1 Turn right onto Scotts Valley Road.

175.2 Ride onto 11th Street.

176.0 Lakeport. End of ride.

Duncan Mills Ramble
Submitted by Karl Kneip

This road bike ride features the Sonoma County Coast and King Ridge Road, taking you through some of the most beautiful scenery in California. With its elevation gain of up to 5,300 feet, it is perfect for hill-climbing specialists. You can visit historic Fort Ross and—for the most part—stay on lightly traveled rural roads.

Type of ride: road bike
Starting point: Duncan Mills
Finishing point: same
Distance: 63.5 miles
Level of difficulty: difficult, with 5,300 cumulative feet of climbing
General terrain: hilly
Traffic conditions: light on rural roads; heavy on State Highway 1 and State Highway 116
Estimated riding time: 5 to 8 hours depending on number of stops at historic sites
Best season/time of day to ride: May through June; September through October; heavy traffic on summer weekends along State Highway 1 and State Highway 116
Points of interest: Stewarts Point, Fort Ross (Russian settlement)
Accommodations and services: all services—except a bike shop— located along the route, but carry food and water for the first 35 miles
Supplemental maps or other information: none

GETTING THERE
On US Highway 101, north of the Golden Gate Bridge, take the River Road exit north of Santa Rosa. Turn left at the stop sign on State Highway

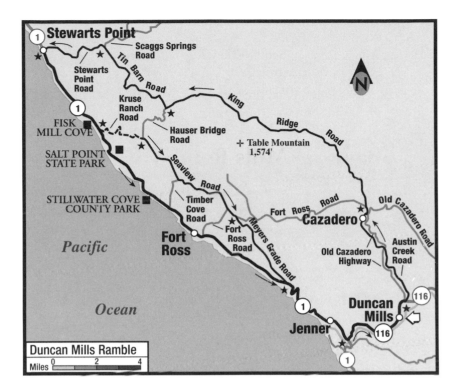

116. At Guerneville, continue straight on Highway 116 west to Duncan Mills. Turn left onto Moscow Road and park away from the shops.

IN THE SADDLE

Start east on Moscow Road for about 0.1 mile, then turn right onto State Highway 116. At the 1-mile mark, turn left onto Austin Creek Road, which becomes the Old Cazadero Highway. In about 7 miles, you will come to the Cazadero Town Store. In another mile, go straight on King Ridge Road at the intersection of Fort Ross Road, Old Cazadero Highway, and King Ridge Road.

The most difficult hill on the route comes after a dozen miles of riding; it averages an 8 percent grade but is only about a mile in length. You will get a view of the copper domes of the Odiyan Buddhist Temple, which is not open to the public.

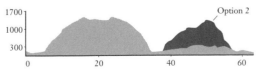

King Ridge Road continues to parallel Mohrhardt Ridge as it winds in a northwesterly direction to its junction with Tin Barn Road at approximately the 25-mile point. Take a right onto Tin Barn Road. In another 4 miles, turn left onto Stewarts Point Road. As you cycle west toward Stewarts Point, cross the famed San Andreas Fault.

At mile 34, join the coastal highway, State Highway 1. The historic Stewarts Point Store, located at this intersection, has been open since 1868.

OPTION 1 (EASY, MORE TRAFFIC)

Turn left (south) onto State Highway 1 towards Fort Ross.

On State Highway 1, pass Fisk Mill Cove (a 0.5-mile walk takes you to a splendid overlook of the coast), Salt Point State Park, and Stillwater Cove County Park.

Fort Ross was once the chief outpost of Russian civilization in California. In the spring of 1812, the Russian-American Fur Company's vessel, the *Chirikov*, deposited a party of fur traders and hunters at the cove. The settlement was planned as a source of food for the fur trading posts in Sitka, Alaska, and farther north. The settlement was named Fort Rossiya (Russia) and was later shortened to Fort Ross.

The Spanish were threatened by the Russian's early success in California and established missions to hem in their eastward expansion from the coast. As the sea otter population was decimated through trapping, Fort Ross fell on hard times; the Russians abandoned the fort and their hopes of California settlements in 1824. The fort and equipment were later purchased by John Sutter; his Sacramento mill was the site of the gold strike that touched off the 1849 gold rush.

Continue on State Highway 1 south to the junction with State Highway 116. There are several sections with no shoulder, and traffic can be busy, especially on spring and summer weekends. Turn off State Highway 1 onto State Highway 116 and follow the Russian River back to Duncan Mills.

OPTION 2 (MORE DIFFICULT, LESS TRAFFIC)

If you would rather add some climbing and lessen the amount of passing traffic, you can return to Duncan Mills on an alternate route. Four miles south of Stewarts Point, turn left onto Kruse Ranch Road, which is gravel. After climbing through a redwood forest for approximately 4

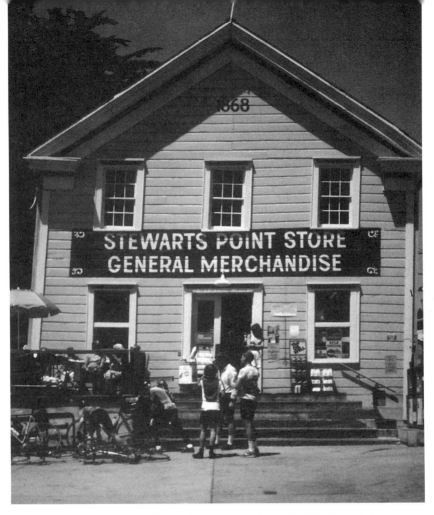

There are many stores along the route. (photo by Karl Kneip)

miles, turn right on Seaview Road and parallel the coast. After joining a 0.5-mile segment of Fort Ross Road (which would take you east to Cazadero), continue straight on Meyers Grade Road. Check your brakes—portions of this grade are steep! At 55 miles, rejoin State Highway 1 for a 5-mile stretch to the junction with State Highway 116. Turn right onto State Highway 116 and return along the Russian River to Duncan Mills.

RIDE GUIDE
    0.0 From Duncan Mills, turn left onto Moscow Road.
    0.1 Turn right onto SR 116.

★   1.0 Turn left onto Austin Creek Road.
      7.0 Cazadero Town Store.
★   8.0 Ride straight onto King Ridge Road.
★   25.0 Turn right onto Tin Barn Road.
★   29.0 Turn left onto Stewarts Point Road.
★   34.0 Stewarts Point. Turn left onto SR 1.

Option 1 (Easy, More Traffic)
      38.1 Continue on SR 1.
      49.0 Fort Ross.
★   60.5 Turn left onto SR 116.
      63.5 Turn right onto Moscow Road. End of ride.

Option 2 (More Difficult, Less Traffic)
★   38.1 Turn left onto Kruse Ranch Road.
★   42.1 Turn right onto Seaview Road.
      49.1 Ride straight onto Fort Ross Road.
★   49.5 Turn right onto Meyers Grade Road.
★   54.5 Turn left onto SR 1.
★   60.5 Turn left onto SR 116.
      63.5 Turn right onto Moscow Road. End of ride.

Winding roads on the Duncan Mills route (photo by Karl Kneip)

Garberville Trek
Submitted by Wally West

The Whittmore Grove of redwoods highlights this 19-mile road bike ride that begins and ends in Garberville. You will get some good views of the South Fork Eel River, but you will have to accomplish some climbing to do it.

Type of ride: road bike
Starting point: Garberville
Finishing point: same
Distance: 18.7 miles
Level of difficulty: moderate
General terrain: hilly
Traffic conditions: generally light, except at rush hour
Estimated riding time: 1.5 to 2.0 hours
Best season/time of day to ride: spring
Points of interest: redwood groves, South Fork Eel River, old ranch homesteads
Accommodations and services: food and water in Garberville; no services along the route
Supplemental maps or other information: none

GETTING THERE
Garberville is located 65 miles southeast of Eureka on US Highway 101. Park at Garberville and ride this loop in a counterclockwise direction for a less hilly ride.

IN THE SADDLE
The town of Garberville is perched on a high terraced bluff on the east side of US Highway 101, overlooking the South Fork Eel River. The town sits in the redwood belt that extends from the extreme southwestern Oregon border to the Santa Lucia Mountains, an area roughly 450 miles long and from 5 to 40 miles in width. This ride will take you through the Whittmore Grove near Redway.

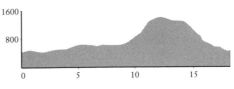

Bear left and cross under US Highway 101, riding along the South Fork Eel River toward Redway. Then bear left on Redwood Drive into Redway. Cross the South Fork Eel River and enter the Whittmore Grove, an extension of the Humboldt Redwoods State Park to the north.

As you exit the Whittmore Grove, Redwood Drive becomes Briceland-Thorne Road. Pass the Briceland Vineyards Winery on your 5-mile jaunt to Briceland, one of those "wide spots in the road" you hear about. Do not miss this wide spot, however, because it is where you turn left (southeast) onto Old Briceland Road.

This is where this ride's climbing begins. You will have a fairly steady 4-mile climb to the top of the ridge, passing an abandoned rancher's homestead and an operating cattle ranch. There are a few breaks in the climb to enjoy the views.

At the 13-mile point in the ride, crest the top of the hills and begin a downhill coast toward Garberville. Watch the speed on the curves and remember that occasionally cars do make use of this road.

This is about the only traffic you will see at this point on the Garberville Trek. (photo by Wally West)

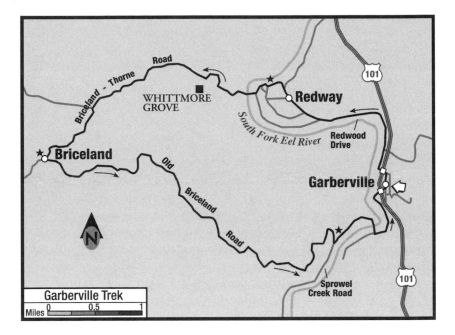

If you keep your speed down, you will get some good views of the South Fork Eel River. This river was named in 1849 by members of the Josiah Gregg party, a government-financed exploratory group. They came upon a small band of Indians who were laden with eels caught in the river, which suggested an appropriate name.

At 15.7 miles, Old Briceland Road ends at a junction with Sprowel Creek Road. The Garberville airport is near the junction. Take a left on Sprowel Creek Road towards Garberville. Cross the South Fork Eel River once more (Camp Kimtu road goes to the right); stay left for the short ride back into Garberville and the end of the ride.

RIDE GUIDE

      0.0 From Garberville, ride north on Redwood Drive.
★   3.2 Redway. Ride onto Briceland-Thorne Road.
★   8.2 Briceland. Turn left onto Old Briceland road.
★ 15.7 Turn left onto Sprowel Creek Road.
    18.1 Garberville. End of ride.

It's all downhill from here. (photo by Wally West)

12 Boont Talk Ride
Submitted by Alan Bloom

This challenging 65-mile loop ride is designed for fit riders, especially those looking to climb some hills. You will pass a number of wineries and several historic towns and maybe pick up some Boontling as well.

Type of ride: road bike
Starting point: Boonville
Finishing point: same

Distance: 65 miles
Level of difficulty: hard
General terrain: hilly; 6,000 feet of steep climbing over length of route
Traffic conditions: light on rural roads; on weekdays less traffic on State Highways 1 and 128
Estimated riding time: 6 to 7 hours
Best season/time of day to ride: spring or fall (a hot ride in the summer)
Points of interest: wineries, Point Arena Lighthouse, Boonville
Accommodations and services: restaurants, groceries, and motel in Boonville; camping at Hendy Woods and Manchester Beach State Parks

GETTING THERE

From San Francisco, take US Highway 101 North (over Golden Gate Bridge) past Santa Rosa and Healdsburg to Cloverdale. Turn left (west) onto State Highway 128 and go 26 miles to Boonville. The Boonville High School parking lot is just to the left on Mountain View Road.

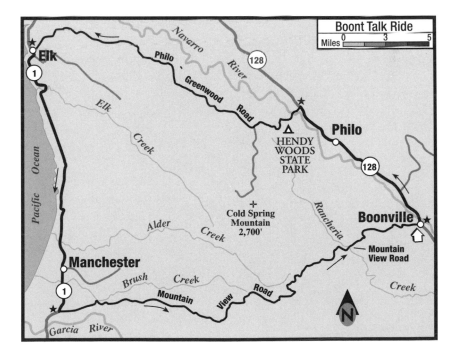

IN THE SADDLE

This ride is named for a regional dialect that over the years evolved in the isolated town of Boonville. The locals came up with words and phrasing that mystified the newcomers that arrived as roads finally led into the area after World War I. The language became known as Boontling, or more commonly by the shortened Boont. The language suggests aspects of English, Spanish, the Celtic languages, French, and even the names of locals. For instance, a telephone might be referred to as a walter levy because Walter Levy was the first person in Boonville to have a phone. You can often find other examples in the *Anderson Valley Advertiser,* the local newspaper.

From Boonville, start riding on a fairly flat State Highway 128. The traffic is low and there are sections with good shoulders (traffic volume picks up on holiday weekends).

A turn onto Philo-Greenwood Road just past Philo will leave the flat road just a pleasant memory—this is where the hills begin. If you have decided to make this a 2-day outing, the Hendy Woods State Park campground is located about 10 miles into the ride, just after you cross the Navarro River on the Philo-Greenwood Road.

The real climbs start right after the state park. The traffic will be light, and it is a beautiful ride, but there is enough challenge to give you a real sense of accomplishment. When you reach the ocean, you will get a breathtaking view as a reward for all of the climbing.

At Elk (also called Greenwood), join State Highway 1 and take a break from the really hilly riding. In its heyday, Elk was a loading center for lumber ships; those operations ceased in the early 1930s. Farther to the south, Manchester and Point Arena were settled as supply centers for the surrounding sheep- and cattle-raising region.

Just southwest of Manchester, the Point Arena Lighthouse stands on a rocky coastal point. Captain George Vancouver anchored the *Discovery* off this promontory in November 1792 and named it *Punto Barro de Arena* (Spanish for "point sand bar"). The first light was

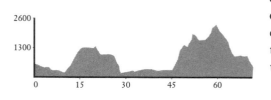

erected here in 1870. The operational lighthouse is open daily from 11:00 A.M. to 2:30 P.M. for self-guided tours.

Just to the north of

California poppies (the state flower), with the Pacific Ocean in the background (photo by Alan Bloom)

Manchester, a state beach offers picnic sites and primitive camping (there is a KOA at Manchester if you like to have more services).

Once you have taken a breather from the hills on State Highway 1, it is time for more. Mountain View Road will burn up any remaining glycogen left in your muscle tissue. These are the most difficult miles of the ride as you head back toward Boonville. The steepest grades are within the first 5 miles or so after the turn onto Mountain View Road. There is a great 3-mile downhill at about mile 49, followed by more ups and downs (mostly ups) all the way back to Boonville.

RIDE GUIDE

      0.0 From Boonville High School parking lot, turn left onto Mountain View Road.

★   0.1 Turn left onto SR 128.

      5.2 Philo

★   8.4 Turn left onto Philo-Greenwood Road.

      8.9 Hendy Woods State Park.

★ 26.0 Elk. Turn left onto SR 1.

   37.7 Manchester.

★ 40.5 Turn left onto Mountain View Road.

   65.0 Boonville High School parking lot. End of ride.

Region 3

Bay Area

A highwheeler sculpture graces a downtown boulevard in Davis
(photo by Gary MacFadden)

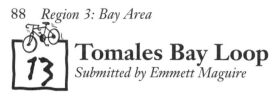

Tomales Bay Loop
Submitted by Emmett Maguire

This is a fun and reasonably easy ride, offering much to see and do along the way. With its close proximity to San Francisco, you will find the roads (especially the sections of State Highway 1) less trafficked on the weekdays.

Type of ride: road bike
Starting point: Nicasio
Finishing point: same
Distance: 50 miles
Level of difficulty: moderate, with a few steep climbs
General terrain: flat to moderately rolling
Traffic conditions: light traffic on two-lane roads; heavier traffic on Sir Francis Drake Boulevard
Estimated riding time: 3 to 4 hours, depending upon stops
Best season/time of day to ride: spring to fall
Points of interest: Tomales Bay, Point Reyes Station, earthquake center, cheese factory
Accommodations and services: cafes, restaurants in towns along the route

GETTING THERE
Begin your ride in the village of Nicasio, located in West Marin County, about 30 miles northwest of the Golden Gate Bridge. Traveling north from San Francisco on US Highway 101, take the Lucas Valley Road turnoff, about 15 miles north of the Golden Gate. Head west on Lucas Valley Road to the junction with Nicasio Valley Road. Turn right on Nicasio Valley Road and travel to Nicasio. Park by the baseball diamond.

IN THE SADDLE
On this 50-mile loop route of moderate difficulty, you will pass near

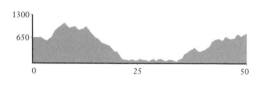

the location that is generally accepted as the point of first California landfall by a European. While the Spanish may have arrived first with Cortés

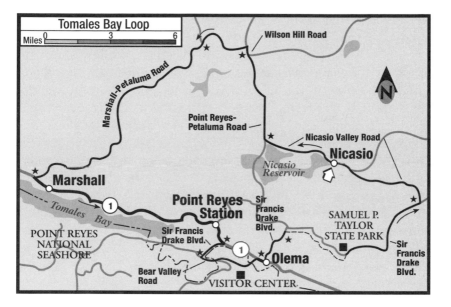

in 1535, the actual first landing is generally credited to the English pirate Sir Francis Drake, who in 1579 anchored the *Golden Hinde* and came ashore at what is today Point Reyes.

For the most part, you will be cycling through low rolling coastal hills, past dairy ranches, and along Tomales Bay, a narrow, fingerlike inlet that early settlers thought resembled a firth in the Scottish Highlands.

In 1863, residents of Nicasio had high hopes of their town becoming the county seat, but they lost out to San Rafael by only one vote. Several of the buildings are more than 100 years old, including the Druids Hall, Post Office, General Store, and Catholic Church.

As you leave Nicasio and turn north onto Nicasio Valley Road, you will pass a one-room schoolhouse that was in use until 1949. Built in 1871, the schoolhouse still has the original blackboards that were transported by ship around Cape Horn, as well as the original school bell in the cupola. Today the schoolhouse is a private residence.

At a ⊤ junction, turn right onto Point Reyes–Petaluma Road. Here you will tackle your first hill of the ride. Several miles beyond the crest pass a cheese factory that specializes in French Brie and Camembert. Some picnic tables and a nice duck pond make this a good spot for a breather and a snack.

The route takes you onto Wilson Hill Road and the Marshall-Petaluma Road. The final portion of the Marshall-Petaluma Road is referred to as Marshall Wall by many local cyclists. While it is steep, to call it a wall would be overstating things a bit. At the top, you will find the climb was worth the effort, because you will get some wonderful vistas of the Pacific Ocean, Point Reyes, Tomales Bay, and the surrounding dairy farming region. To top off the view, there is a terrific downhill to State Highway 1.

Pedal toward Point Reyes Station and follow the sea-blue waters of Tomales Bay. The name Tomales is thought to be a Spanish corruption of the Coast Miwok Indian word *tamal* for "bay." To the west, across the bay, are the hills of the Point Reyes National Seashore. Your route winds past fishing docks and commercial oyster beds.

A nice spot for a break (photo by Emmett Maguire)

After tiny Tomales Bay State Park (check out the osprey nest on a phone pole that once stood along the highway but was moved by the power company to give the nesting birds more privacy), coast into Point Reyes Station. This town, complete with bakery and deli, makes a great lunch stop. If you happen to be around at noon, you will discover that even the town's noon whistle underscores the importance of the dairy industry—instead of a fire siren or factory whistle, the noon signal is a loud bovine "MOOOOO." (The recording was donated by Marin County resident and special effects wizard George Lucas.)

After a jaunt on Bear Valley Road, you will come to the Point Reyes National Seashore Visitor Center. There is a short "earthquake walk" that you can do in about 10 minutes. The highlight of the walk is a chance to straddle the infamous San Andreas Fault at the epicenter of the 1906 earthquake that wreaked so much havoc on San Francisco.

Sir Francis Drake Boulevard and a 3.5-mile bike path through groves of towering redwoods and bay trees lead you to Samuel P. Taylor State Park. Then it is back to Nicasio Valley Road. On the final stretch into Nicasio you will pass through numerous attractive horse ranches.

RIDE GUIDE

  0.0 From Nicasio, ride north on Nicasio Valley Road.
★ 3.3 Turn right onto Point Reyes–Petaluma Road.
★ 7.7 Turn left onto Wilson Hill Road.
★ 10.4 Bear left onto Marshall-Petaluma Road.
★ 21.4 Turn left onto SR 1.
 31.1 Point Reyes Station.
★ 32.0 Turn right onto Sir Francis Drake Boulevard.
★ 32.7 Turn left onto Bear Valley Road.
 34.5 Turn right into Point Reyes National Seashore Visitor Center.
 35.0 Leave park headquarters same way you entered.
★ 35.6 Turn right onto SR 1.
 35.7 Olema. Turn left onto Sir Francis Drake Boulevard.
★ 37.5 Turn right onto bike path.
 41.0 Samuel P. Taylor State Park. Continue on Sir Francis Drake Boulevard.
★ 45.8 Turn left onto Nicasio Valley Road.
 50.0 Nicasio. End of ride.

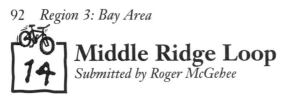

Middle Ridge Loop
Submitted by Roger McGehee

This is a short (9.5-mile) but difficult mountain bike ride in Henry Coe State Park. It features some great single-tracks as well as several steep climbs and descents.

Type of ride: mountain bike
Starting point: Henry W. Coe State Park Headquarters
Finishing point: same
Distance: 9.5 miles
Level of difficulty: hard
General terrain: steep climbs and ascents
Traffic conditions: none (other than hikers and other cyclists)
Estimated riding time: 2.0 to 2.5 hours
Best season/time of day to ride: spring through fall
Points of interest: secluded backcountry riding
Accommodations and services: services only at park headquarters; no food available
Supplemental maps or other information: map available at park headquarters

GETTING THERE
This ride is based in the Henry W. Coe State Park, located directly east of the city of Morgan Hill in the Santa Clara Valley on US Highway 101 south of San Francisco. Take the East Dunne Avenue exit from US Highway 101 at Morgan Hill and head east (inland). At the top of the first hill, look for the sign to Henry W. Coe State Park. You will follow a narrow, winding road to the park entrance.

IN THE SADDLE
There are several good single-track rides in Henry W. Coe State Park. Check in at the park headquarters for a current map. Note that the trails near the headquarters, even though they look like good single-track rides, are closed to bicycles. Most of these closed trails are clearly marked. Also note that all of the park trails are closed for 48 hours after each heavy storm, which is judged as 0.5 inch or more of precipitation. This keeps the trails from becoming rutted and damaged.

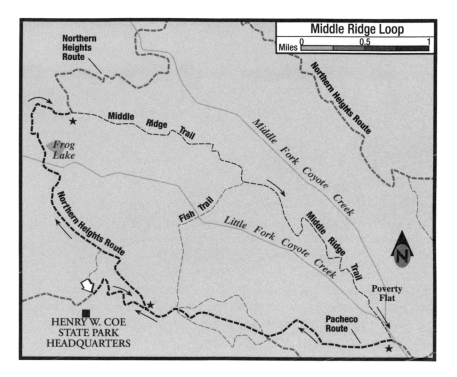

Henry W. Coe State Park is the largest state park in northern California, with just over 79,000 acres. It includes a 23,000-acre state-designated wilderness area. The terrain throughout the park is rugged and varied. Gentle ridge tops are separated by deep canyons; you will get a sampling of each during the ride. There is a great deal of climbing, so allow a couple of hours and take plenty of water with you, because there is none available en route.

From the park headquarters, ride east onto a dirt road toward Northern Heights Route. At 0.7 mile, turn left onto Northern Heights Route toward Frog Lake.

You will be passing through a number of environments during this short ride. Grassland and oak savanna cover the ridge tops in the park. Ponderosa pine marks the higher ridges on the western side of the park, while coast live oaks and chaparral cover the warmer, drier south-facing slopes. Big leaf maples and alders line the streams.

You will reach Frog Lake at the 2-mile point in the ride. Continue on Northern Heights Route to the junction with the Middle Ridge

Trail. At first, this route gently rises and falls along a grassy, open ridge line, through groves of large manzanita. After several miles of gentle riding, the trail gets much steeper, more technical, and more exposed. There are places you will want to walk your bike, and that inclination is not discouraged.

The Middle Ridge Trail will take you to Poverty Flat (at approximately 6.8 miles). Turn right onto Pacheco Route for a climb out of the canyon. Join the Coit Route on your way back to the dirt road leading to the park headquarters.

RIDE GUIDE

    0.0 From Henry W. Coe State Park Headquarters, ride east on dirt road.

★ 0.7 Turn left onto Northern Heights Route.

    2.1 Frog Lake.

★ 2.7 Turn right onto Middle Ridge Trail.

★ 6.8 Poverty Flat. Turn right onto Pacheco Route.

★ 8.8 Turn left onto unnamed dirt road to return to the Park Headquarters.

    9.5 Henry W. Coe State Park Headquarters. End of ride.

Wilder Ridge Loop
Submitted by Scott Harriger

This 6.6-mile loop will take you through canyons of redwoods, past exceptional views, and on intermittent climbs and stretches of flat-to-rolling terrain.

Type of ride: mountain bike
Starting point: Wilder Ranch State Park parking lot
Finishing point: same
Distance: 6.6 miles
Level of difficulty: moderate
General terrain: varies
Traffic conditions: none; route is on single-track trails
Estimated riding time: 1 hour

Best season/time of day to ride: May through October
Points of interest: redwood-filled canyons, wildlife
Accommodations and services: no services other than rest rooms; groceries available nearby, outside park
Supplemental maps or other information: map showing mountain biking trails at Wilder Ranch State Park, available at park entrance station; Krebs cycling map for the area, available at local bicycle shops

GETTING THERE

The entrance to Wilder Ranch State Park is on the south side of State Highway 1, approximately 1.7 miles northwest of Santa Cruz. The park entrance fee is $6 per car. There is a parking lot/turnout just east of the park entrance where you can park and avoid the entrance fee, but the area is not patrolled. Damage to cars and thefts have been reported

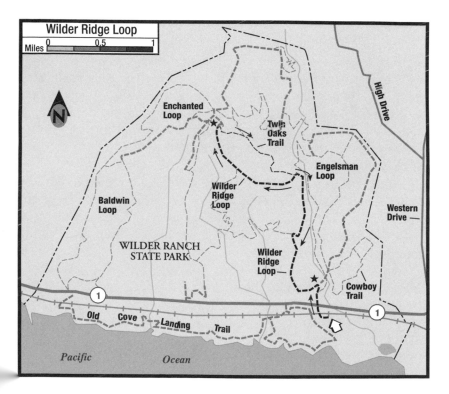

by cyclists using this area, so park here at your own risk. If you do, lock valuables in the trunk.

IN THE SADDLE

As a state park, Wilder Ranch differs from the norm. The primary purpose of the park is to serve as a demonstration museum showing life on a coastal dairy farm. Before tourism became the region's mainstay, dairying was an important element in the economy of Santa Cruz and the surrounding area.

The park and ranch buildings sustained significant damage from the October 1989 Loma Prieta earthquake. While most of the media attention centered on the Bay Area to the north, the epicenter of the quake was only a few miles from Wilder Ranch State Park, at nearby Forest of Nisene Marks State Park. Downtown Santa Cruz lost a number of historic buildings during that quake.

The terrain at the 2,000-acre park varies from grassy benchlands and bluffs along the beach to deep canyons filled with redwoods. This short ride will give you a sampling of the park's varied ecosystems.

From the park entrance and ranch house area, pass under State Highway 1 through a tunnel. Then make a sharp left turn and begin heading up a short but steep hill. During the early portion of the ride, you will be faced with intermittent climbs and flat to rolling terrain. At the junction with Twin Oaks Trail, go left to stay on Wilder Ridge Loop. More climbing after the turn at the junction will take you to a fine viewpoint of the surrounding beaches, the city of Santa Cruz, and Monterey Bay.

From this point your ride will be mostly along the elevation of Wilder Ridge. See the Ride Guide for turns that will keep you on the loop. Numerous other trails intersect the loop trail; if you have time, explore these trails that sport names such as Zane Grey Trail, Horseman's Trail, and Enchanted Loop.

At the top of Wilder Ridge Loop, turn right onto Twin Oaks Trail, which will take you back to the junction you passed earlier. Then it is down through familiar terrain and back to the park headquarters.

RIDE GUIDE

    0.0 From parking lot, ride to ranch house area and then
          through tunnel under SR 1.

★ 0.6 Turn left onto Wilder Ridge Loop.
    1.4 Bear right to continue on Wilder Ridge Loop.
    2.2 Bear left to continue on Wilder Ridge Loop.
    3.2 Bear right to continue on Wilder Ridge Loop.
★ 3.3 Turn right onto Twin Oaks Trail.
    4.4 Ride onto Wilder Ridge Loop.
    5.2 Bear left to continue on Wilder Ridge Loop.
★ 6.0 Bear right to continue on Wilder Ridge Loop.
    6.6 Parking lot. End of ride.

A good spot for a dip near Point Reyes (photo by Gary Macfadden)

Pescadero Loop
Submitted by Marianne Tamm

16

This 44-mile road ride includes some steep sections and one highly trafficked section but is suitable for beginners with some experience. A shorter option of 28 miles follows mostly little-trafficked roads.

Type of ride: road bike
Starting point: Pescadero
Finishing point: same

Distance: 44 miles
Level of difficulty: moderate
General terrain: hilly
Traffic conditions: light on rural roads, very heavy on State Highway 1
Estimated riding time: 4 to 5 hours
Best season/time of day to ride: spring through fall
Points of interest: Pescadero, Pigeon Point Lighthouse
Accommodations and services: food at Pescadero and stage stop; youth hostel at lighthouse

GETTING THERE

Begin and end this loop ride in Pescadero, located approximately 17 miles south of Half Moon Bay on State Highway 1 (south of San Francisco). Turn east (inland) off Highway 1 onto Pescadero Road and follow it for about 2 miles to Pescadero. You can park in the downtown area, where there is a store, restaurant, and bakery for stocking up on picnic provisions. The ride begins on Stage Road, past the bakery and a small church.

IN THE SADDLE

Pescadero (Indian for "fishing place") was named for Pescadero Creek's once plentiful supply of trout, but the town was settled predominantly by Portuguese emigrants who never made it a business to either catch or sell fish. Instead, the area's inhabitants of European descent specialized largely in the growing of artichokes, brussels sprouts, and other crops.

Head north out of Pescadero on Stage Road, which is actually what remains of the old coast highway. At a small cemetery on the outskirts of town, the road narrows, and you will cycle through pasturelands and eucalyptus groves with little traffic. The road climbs and descends several low ridges, taking you to San Gregorio.

A once-thriving stage stop at the intersection of State Highway 84 and Stage Road is today marked by a small country store. Turn east (right) onto State Highway 84, a wide-shouldered, two-lane highway. The gentle 7-mile grade will take you into a mixed forest of pine, bay, and some redwoods. In the distance, catch glimpses of the Santa Cruz mountains.

Just before entering La Honda, turn right onto Pescadero Road. After approximately 1 mile of gradual climbing through a wide, forest-lined

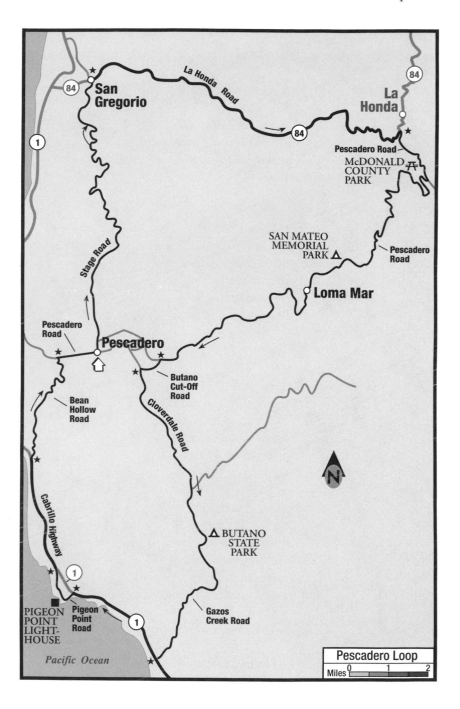

Pigeon Point Lighthouse (photo by Marianne Tamm)

road, Pescadero Road meets Alpine Road (this is at approximately mile 16 in the ride). Be sure to continue to the right, crossing the bridge. The road narrows and starts to climb more steeply, but the views of the surrounding redwood forest more than make up for the effort. After about 0.5 mile of climbing, cross the boundary of McDonald County Park. There is a turn-in for rest rooms and water and a beautiful picnic area among the redwoods.

The steep climb lasts for another 2 miles, to the summit of Haskins Hill. You are then rewarded with a steep downhill to the entrance of San Mateo Memorial Park, after approximately 3 miles. There is a complete campground facility here, equipped with showers, a small camp store during the camping season, water, and picnic tables. It is another nice lunch stop.

The road continues gradually downhill to Loma Mar, a small community with a general store and a restaurant. The redwood forest will be left behind as you continue westward into the low coastal hills. At mile 27, the Butano Cut-Off Road intersects Pescadero Road on the left. Here you can return to Pescadero for a shortened ride of approximately 28 miles. Otherwise, take the Butano Cut-Off Road to the left, which takes you to Cloverdale Road.

Turn left onto this wide-shouldered road with light traffic. In about 4 miles, pass the turnoff for Butano State Park (at mile 31). Camping is available year-round in this park. There are also rest rooms, water, and picnic tables for day use. Cloverdale Road continues over the rolling coastal hills. There is a swooping downhill run to Gazos Creek Road. Stay right, following Gazos Creek downstream through beautiful scenery.

The quiet will be interrupted at the intersection of Gazos Creek Road and State Highway 1. The highway has wide shoulders, but you can expect high-speed traffic for the next 2.5 miles. Exercise extreme caution along the highway and in making your left-hand turn onto Pigeon Point Road, toward the Pigeon Point Lighthouse.

The lighthouse has a dramatic setting on a rocky bluff above the pounding surf of the Pacific. The point is named for the Boston clipper *Carrier Pigeon*, which was wrecked on the headland in May 1853. The lighthouse was constructed in 1872 and today is an American Youth Hostel. There are tours of the lighthouse, but the hours are limited.

Time for a snack (photo by Marianne Tamm)

Continue north along Pigeon Point Road, a narrow beachfront access road, which will lead you back to State Highway 1. Continue north on State Highway 1 for 3 miles and watch for the point where Bean Hollow Road veers off to the right (at about mile 40). This narrow, quiet road will be a welcome relief after the rush of traffic on State Highway 1. It climbs gradually for a mile through artichoke fields and provides some great views of the ocean.

After coasting down to the junction with Pescadero Road, turn right and head back into Pescadero, passing local produce stands. If you are hungry, one of the town specialties is artichoke-garlic bread. Try a piece!

RIDE GUIDE
    0.0 From Pescadero, ride north on Stage Road.
★ 7.3 San Gregorio. Turn right onto SR 84 (La Honda Road).
★ 14.9 Turn right onto Pescadero Road.
★ 16.0 Bear right to continue on Pescadero Road.
    22.2 Loma Mar.
★ 26.9 Turn left onto Butano Cut-Off Road.
★ 27.4 At т, turn left onto Cloverdale Road.
    31.1 Butano State Park.

32.4 Route becomes Gazos Creek Road.
★ 34.4 Turn right onto SR 1.
★ 37.0 Turn left onto Pigeon Point Road.
★ 37.3 At ⊤, turn left onto SR 1 (Cabrillo Highway).
★ 40.1 Bear right onto Bean Hollow Road.
★ 42.8 Turn right onto Pescadero Road.
43.5 Pescadero. End of ride.

Occidental Loop
Submitted by Alan and Jane Baron

You will pass through windswept coastal highlands, gain spectacular
ocean views, and explore quaint seaside towns. (If you are looking for
an easier ride, be sure to stay on the Bodega Highway when returning
to Occidental.)

Type of ride: road bike
Starting point: Occidental
Finishing point: same
Distance: 26 miles
Level of difficulty: easy
General terrain: moderately rolling
Traffic conditions: light traffic on two-lane roads
Estimated riding time: 2 to 3 hours
Best season/time of day to ride: spring through fall
Points of interest: botanical gardens, redwoods, Bodega Bay (site of
    Hitchcock's *The Birds*)
Accommodations and services: food and water available along the
    route

GETTING THERE
From San Francisco, drive north over the Golden Gate Bridge to Santa
Rosa. Turn left onto State Highway 12 (Sebastopol Road) and go 10
miles to Sebastopol. Take Bodega Highway west out of Sebastopol; at
the junction with Bohemian Highway, turn right onto Bohemian Highway and follow it 4 miles to Occidental.

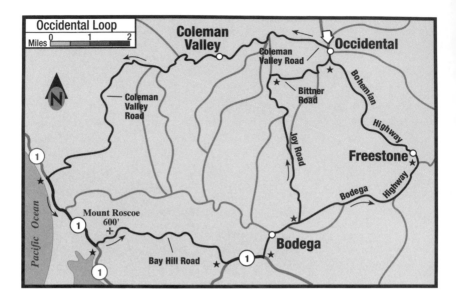

IN THE SADDLE

The ride begins in Occidental, at the junction of Bohemian Highway and Coleman Valley Road. The town of Occidental is situated in the midst of towering redwood and Douglas-fir forests. Being so close to San Francisco, the town is a popular summer destination, because it does not share the cool, foggy days that mark Bay Area summers. You will probably find it sunny and clear.

Cycle west up Coleman Valley Road, leaving the Occidental Valley, and gain 460 feet in elevation. If the "Open" sign is out, be sure to visit Western Hill Rare Plants, a unique botanical garden.

You will see moderate-sized redwoods and bay laurels that gradually yield to cottonwoods along meandering Coleman Valley Creek. Climb through intersecting meadows of mustard flowers and rattail reeds to a plateau where you will begin to feel (and appreciate) the ocean breezes.

The now-dense redwoods and eucalyptus will give way to rocky outcroppings and copses of scrub oak, where sheep roam the hillsides. This was originally dairy cow country, but

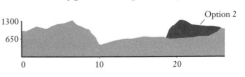

during World War II, the coastal blackout control forbade the ranchers to show any lights during the dark milking hours. Rather than attempt to lightproof their large old milking barns, the ranchers turned to sheep.

A sweeping downhill will take you to Coast Highway (State Highway 1), where you will turn south. Note: This is the most trafficked section of the route, especially during the summer months. You will pass a number of state beaches, as well as the majestic Monterey pines.

At Bay Hill Road, turn left, climb a moderate grade, and gain a good vantage point of Bodega Bay, a commercial fishing village, and Bodega Head. Bay Hill Road will take you back to Coast Highway and then to a turn that leads into Bodega.

Bodega and Bodega Bay are today best known as the sites for the filming of Alfred Hitchcock's *The Birds*. If you have seen the film, you will probably recognize the church and schoolhouse, both important scenic anchors in the movie. Two hundred years before Hitchcock arrived, when the Spanish navigator Juan Francisco de la Bodega y Cuadra sailed into the bay in 1776, the bay was inhabited by the Miwok Indians. (Fortunately for us the Spanish only used a portion of the navigator's handle when naming the town.)

Tailwinds prevail on this part of the coastal highway. (photo by Jane Baron)

The schoolhouse from Hitchcock's *The Birds* (photo by Jane Baron)

Bodega is at roughly the halfway point in the ride, so it makes a good stop for a picnic lunch or a restaurant visit.

Take Bodega Highway out of Bodega to Joy Road. Here you have the option for an easy or more difficult ride back to Occidental.

OPTION 1 (EASY)

Continue east on Bodega Highway. Pass the Watson Schoolhouse, another nice site for a picnic. The route rejoins Bohemian Highway back to Occidental. Along the way you will pass the little village of Freestone, named for a type of sandstone that was easily quarried nearby. Freestone was one of the many stops along the Northwest Pacific Coast Railroad (circa 1876), which carried hundreds of San Francisco tourists to Freestone and other small communities and not a few redwood logs to the mill. One of the early Russian settlements in California was near Freestone. The Russians, hoping to bolster the food supplies for their Alaskan colonies, selected Bodega Bay as their shipping point for agricultural products grown at farming settlements in Freestone and nearby Jenner, Salmon Creek, and Sebastopol.

Continue north on Bohemian Highway and return to Occidental. (The final tour distance on this main route is 26 miles.)

OPTION 2 (MORE DIFFICULT)

If looking for a workout, you will be rewarded for choosing this route with some extra scenic views. Joy Road is also less trafficked than the Bodega Highway, and the route shaves a couple of miles from the total trip distance. From the intersection of Joy Road and Bodega Highway, climb 800 feet in less than 3 miles. After the summit, Joy Road gradually drops down to meet Bittner Road; turn right onto Bittner Road through shady stands of redwood and eucalyptus. Meet Bohemian Highway as it enters Occidental. (The final tour distance with this alternate route is just under 24 miles.)

RIDE GUIDE

0.0 From corner of Coleman Valley Road and Bohemian Highway in Occidental, ride west on Coleman Valley Road.

1.8 Bear right to continue on Coleman Valley Road.

★ 10.1 Turn left onto SR 1.

★ 12.3 Turn left onto Bay Hill Road.
★ 16.1 Turn left onto SR 1.
★ 17.0 Turn left onto Bodega Highway.
　 17.6 Bodega. Continue east on Bodega Highway.

Option 1 (Easy)
　 18.4 Continue east on Bodega Highway.
　 19.8 Watson Schoolhouse.
★ 22.1 Turn left onto Bohemian Highway.
　 22.5 Freestone.
　 26.0 Occidental. End of ride.

Option 2 (More Difficult)
★ 18.4 Turn left onto Joy Road.
★ 21.9 Turn right onto Bittner Road.
★ 23.1 Turn left onto Bohemian Highway.
　 23.6 Occidental. End of ride.

Bovine Bakery Ride
Submitted by Sandy Zirulnik

This ride offers a great variety of northern California scenery, including rolling hills, redwood forests, ocean views, and bay habitat.

Type of ride: road bike
Starting point: Ross
Finishing point: same
Distance: 54 miles
Level of difficulty: moderate
General terrain: gently rolling (some steep but short) climbs
Traffic conditions: nearly entirely rural two-lane roads with light traffic; begins and ends in a business district; in Samuel Taylor Park, traffic heavy on summer weekend afternoons (bypass about two-thirds of this busy park section on a paved bicycle path)
Estimated riding time: 3 to 4 hours

Alpine Lake Reservoir (photo by Sandy Zirulnik)

Best season/time of day to ride: any time, but spring through fall is best

Points of interest: Point Reyes, earthquake self-guided tour

Accommodations and services: food and water available along the route

GETTING THERE

This ride begins at Ross Commons in Ross, near San Anselmo. Twelve miles north of San Francisco, exit US Highway 101 onto Sir Francis Drake Boulevard and head west to the town of Ross. Turn left at the Bufano statue and immediately left again to enter the parking area in Ross Commons.

IN THE SADDLE

Head north out of Ross Commons, turning left onto Lagunitas Road for one block, then right onto Shady Lane. Ride to the end of Shady Lane (approximately 0.5 mile) and turn right onto Bolinas Avenue. Ride

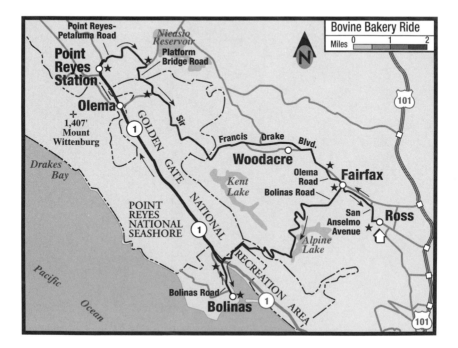

A well-deserved break (photo by Sandy Zirulnik)

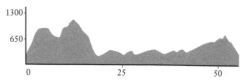

ne block and turn left onto an Anselmo Avenue. This ill take you through the an Anselmo business disict, which tends to be "cyclist aware." Bear left (at 1.3 miles) to stay on San Anselmo Avenue at the north end of town. Bear right at 1.5 miles and right again at 1.9 miles to remain on San Anselmo Avenue. At 2.2 miles, follow the bike route signs onto Lansdale Avenue.

Next you will navigate through the town of Fairfax. Bear left onto Center Avenue at 2.6 miles; Center becomes Broadway in Fairfax. Turn left onto Bolinas Road at 2.9 miles. That is it for the navigating for a while.

Bolinas Road takes you away from the business of civilization as quickly as you can climb the fairly steep hills through live oak terrain. You will get some sweeping views and may see deer, turkey vultures, hawks, and other wildlife.

At about the 8-mile point, descend through the forest to Alpine Lake. Stop on top of the dam and enjoy the view. In the spring, the reservoir is full, and water will be cascading down the spillway on your right.

For the next 5 miles or so, climb quite steeply through beautiful redwood forests to the junction with Ridgecrest. At the top of the climb, bear right to stay on Bolinas Road, which descends in a number of switchbacks. Do not get too carried away with speed or you will miss a number of fine ocean views. Also keep watch for the occasional ascending car.

At approximately 18 miles, Bolinas Road joins State Highway 1. You can take a quick side trip spur of approximately 2 miles (4 miles roundtrip) into Bolinas or turn right onto State Highway 1 toward Olema. This is a nice ride through bay habitat into Bolinas, and there are food services available. The directions into Bolinas are noted in the Ride Guide.

Mild rolling hills will keep things interesting as you pedal the 9 miles to Olema. If you have time, turn left onto Bear Valley Road 0.25 mile north of Olema and tour the Point Reyes National Seashore Visitor Center. A self-guided earthquake trail takes you along the San Andreas Fault.

Continue north to Point Reyes Station on State Highway 1. This is a small, scenic town with restaurants, a market, and a bakery. At the north end of town, turn right, staying with State Highway 1. Climb a short hill and turn right onto Point Reyes–Petaluma Road. You are about 35 miles into the trip at this point.

Turn right at the stop sign onto Platform Bridge Road at 37.8 miles and roll through a little canyon to the junction with Sir Francis Drake Boulevard at about 41 miles.

Now you have a choice. About 30 feet before the intersection with Sir Francis Drake Boulevard, you can make a right over an old bridge. If you pass under Sir Francis Drake Boulevard and onto a paved bike path, you will be able to ride through the campgrounds and a heavily forested area of Samuel Taylor State Park, paralleling and eventually ending up back at Sir Francis Drake Boulevard. Be careful on this path when traffic is present; a short distance within the park the road is narrow with no shoulders. Your other choice, if you are in a hurry, is to avoid the park by turning left onto Sir Francis Drake Boulevard. You will climb a nice hill and ride faster.

Follow Sir Francis Drake back to Fairfax, passing through the small towns of Lagunitas, Forest Knolls, San Geronimo, and Woodacre. At just over 50 miles, bear right onto Olema Road at the bike route sign and head into Fairfax. Then retrace your earlier path to Ross Commons.

RIDE GUIDE

0.0 From Ross Commons in Ross, head north and turn left onto Lagunitas Road.

0.1 Turn right onto Shady Lane.

0.5 Turn right onto Bolinas Avenue.

0.6 Turn left onto San Anselmo Avenue.

1.3 Bear left to continue on San Anselmo Avenue.

1.5 Bear right to continue on San Anselmo Avenue.

1.9 Bear right to continue on San Anselmo Avenue.

2.2 Follow the bike route signs onto Lansdale Avenue.

2.6 Bear left onto Center Avenue. In Fairfax, Center Avenue becomes Broadway.

★ 2.9 Turn left onto Bolinas Road.

3.3 Bear left to continue on Bolinas Road.

★ 17.9 Cross SR 1.

18.1 Turn left to continue on Bolinas Road.

19.2 Turn left to continue on Bolinas Road.

20.8 Bolinas. Continue on Bolinas Road.

★ 21.0 Turn around and ride north on Bolinas Road.
★ 22.7 Turn left onto SR 1.
    31.5 Olema.
★ 35.0 Turn right onto Point Reyes–Petaluma Road.
★ 37.8 At stop sign, turn right onto Platform Bridge Road.
★ 40.7 Turn left onto Sir Francis Drake Boulevard.
★ 50.3 Bear right onto Olema Road.
★ 51.2 Turn right onto Sir Francis Drake Boulevard.
    51.4 Turn right onto Broadway, which becomes Center Avenue.
    52.0 Ride onto Lansdale Avenue.
    52.3 Ride onto San Anselmo Avenue.
    52.7 Bear left to continue on San Anselmo Avenue.
    52.9 Bear right to continue on San Anselmo Avenue.
    53.6 Turn right onto Bolinas Avenue.
    53.7 Turn left onto Shady Lane.
    54.1 Turn left onto Lagunitas Road.
    54.2 Ross Commons. End of ride.

Davis Romp

Submitted by Steven Anderson

This road biking loop begins and ends in Davis, home of the University of California at Davis (UCD). Davis is well-known among bicyclists as being one of the most progressive cycling towns in the United States. Its bicycle and pedestrian facilities are truly first class, so be sure to allow some time to cycle around the town and try them out.

Type of ride: road bike
Starting point: Davis
Finishing point: same
Distance: 63 miles
Level of difficulty: easy to moderate (one steep climb to Lake Berryessa)
General terrain: flat
Traffic conditions: light to moderate on rural two-lane roads
Estimated riding time: 4 to 5 hours
Best season/time of day to ride: spring

One of the few locals who doesn't ride a bike (photo by Steven Anderson)

Points of interest: Davis historic homes tour, solar facility, Lake Berryessa

Accommodations and services: Davis has all services; food and water in Winters

Supplemental maps or other information: historic homes cycling tour brochure at Davis Chamber of Commerce, 228 B. Street, (510) 756-5160

GETTING THERE

Davis is 15 miles west of Sacramento on Interstate 80. Park in one of the downtown community parking lots. The ride starts at the corner of 2nd Street and Pole Line Road.

IN THE SADDLE

This 63-mile route travels over fairly flat country, except for the short climb up to Lake Berryessa. The return to Davis is along the quiet back roads and bike paths paralleling Putah Creek. Summers in the Davis area are generally hot and dry. You might want to try this route in the spring, when the surrounding fields are at their greenest.

The town of Davis is named for Jerome C. Davis, an early settler who by 1856 had 400 acres planted in wheat and barley, huge herds of livestock, and orchards and vineyards. Quite a setting for the state's agricultural school.

As you leave Davis on the Pole Line Road and travel toward Winters, you will pass through some very productive farmland that supports tomatoes, corn, barley, and alfalfa. There is a lot of irrigation in the area, especially for the rice paddies, which require flooding.

The route includes a short "pigtail" section to Monticello Dam and Lake Berryessa. You can do a shorter version of this ride by forgoing the Lake Berryessa section and returning to Davis after entering Winters. The ride distance is then shortened to approximately 42 miles.

There is one slightly tricky turn that you have to watch for where the "pigtail" begins and ends. When leaving Lake Berryessa on State Highway 128 to return to Davis, watch for Pleasants Valley Road (Road 86). A small grocery store marks the junction of Pleasants Valley Road and State Highway 128. Cross the bridge on Pleasants Valley Road and then watch for a turn to the left within 1 mile onto Putah Creek Road. This road will take you back toward Davis, through orchards of almond, cherry, and walnut and beneath the drooping, feathery branches of gray-green tamarisks.

At the junction of Stevenson Bridge Road and Russell Boulevard (mile 56), ride onto a well-maintained bike path beautifully lined with trees. Follow the bike path for the final 5 miles back to the University of California at Davis campus and Davis. Use caution as you approach Davis on the path: It is used by joggers and pedestrians as well as by cyclists.

Once back in Davis, drop by the Chamber of Commerce to pick up a brochure that details a historic architecture tour, the Davis Historic Bike Tour, designed specifically to be enjoyed from the seat of a bicycle. There are 26 sites if you take the entire tour; the brochure includes a clearly drawn map keyed to the sites. If you are sticking around town for a day or two, also request a copy of the Davis Bike Map.

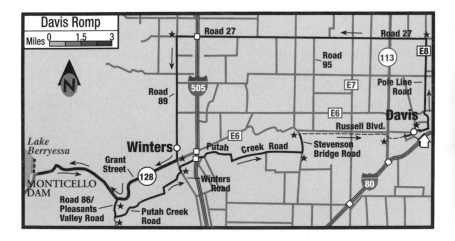

RIDE GUIDE

    0.0 From Sudwerk Restaurant, turn left onto Pole Line Road.

★   5.2 Turn left onto Road 27.

★ 18.6 Turn left onto Road 89.

   24.2 Winters.

★ 25.4 Turn right onto Grant Street (SR 128).

   35.3 Top of Monticello Dam. Turn around and retrace route to Road 86.

★ 40.9 Turn right onto Road 86 (Pleasants Valley Road).

★ 42.0 Turn left onto Putah Creek Road.

★ 46.8 Turn left onto Winters Road.

   47.1 Turn right onto Putah Creek Road.

★ 54.3 Turn left onto Stevenson Bridge Road.

★ 55.7 Turn right onto bike path paralleling Russell Boulevard.

   59.1 Davis.

   60.5 Turn right onto bike path to University of California at Davis.

   61.0 Ride straight onto Third Street.

   62.8 Turn right onto "L" Street.

   63.3 Sudwerk Restaurant. End of ride.

Tomato fields (photo by Steven Anderson)

Mount Tam Climb
Submitted by Andrew Davidson

This is a road ride of moderate difficulty on a mountain that is well-known in the cycling world as the reputed birthplace of the mountain bike. It is a very scenic ride, with sweeping views of the Pacific Ocean and the Bay Area.

Type of ride: road bike
Starting point: San Anselmo
Finishing point: same
Distance: 38 miles
Level of difficulty: moderate
General terrain: hilly on outbound leg, mostly downhill on return
Traffic conditions: heavy on weekends, especially in summer
Estimated riding time: 4 to 5 hours (allows time for enjoying the scenery and eating at a leisurely pace)
Best season/time of day to ride: mid-spring through early autumn; avoid busy summer weekends
Points of interest: Mount Tamalpais observation area; views of San Francisco and Bay Area
Accommodations and services: food on weekends at top of ride; fewer services on weekdays; Fairfax and Mill Valley full of places to eat
Supplemental maps or other information: AAA map for San Rafael, San Anselmo, Fairfax, and Mill Valley

GETTING THERE

This road ride starts in San Anselmo, which is about 20 minutes north of San Francisco on US Highway 101. Take the San Rafael exit off US Highway 101. Pass through the communities of Greenbrae, Kentfield, and Ross before reaching San Anselmo, approximately 3 miles west of the highway. At the intersection of Sir Francis Drake Boulevard and 4th Avenue, take a sharp left onto Center Boulevard; at the stop sign, take another left onto Bridge Avenue. Cross the small bridge, which ends at a T at San Anselmo Avenue and find a parking spot (you may want to park on a side street rather than on the busier San Anselmo Avenue). See Ride 18 for suggestions for parking at Ross Commons.

Just one of the impressive views from the climb up Mount Tam
(photo by John Stein)

IN THE SADDLE

As a route for providing scenic vistas, this ride cannot be beat. However,
the vistas mean that the route is in the open a great deal. Do not forget
the sunblock and plenty of water. Also, be ready for varied climates. A
windbreaker is a good idea, especially for the return ride downhill.

Beginning at the intersection of San Anselmo Avenue and Center
Boulevard, follow the green and white Bike Route signs that keep you
on San Anselmo. Stay on this road to Landsdale Station Park intersection at just under 1 mile. Turn onto Landsdale Avenue, still paralleling
Center Boulevard. Enter Fairfax.

Landsdale Avenue ends at the intersection of Belmonte and Broadway (at 1.3 miles). Turn left onto Broadway, which will take you through
downtown Fairfax (a bike shop is on your left if you need service). Take
a left onto Bolinas Road at 1.6 miles. This is the last chance to check
your water bottles. You face a climb of 2,300 feet, so check now.

At the stop sign, veer to the left. Your climbing begins shortly after
Bolinas Road becomes Fairfax-Bolinas Road somewhere in this section.
It is a two-lane, curvy road without much (if any) shoulder. The climb
is not too severe.

At 4.2 miles, the road levels as you pass the Meadow Club golf course and go through an access gate. Here you enter the Mount Tamalpais Watershed. (Tamalpais is pronounced Tam-ul-PIE-iss, or simply call

it Mount Tam for short.) Fairfax-Bolinas Road may be closed from time to time due to fire danger. It is a good idea to call the Marin Municipal Water District (415-488-9577) prior to your ride to check on the road's status.

At 5.4 miles, pass the Pine Mountain parking area. This is a popular parking place for cyclists who are looking for less of an outing than those who started at the bottom of the climb. From the parking area, you will get a speedy descent for the next mile. Off to your left is Alpine Lake; farther to the south you can see the eastern peak of Mount Tamalpais.

After the steep downhill, begin a more gradual descent, coasting through stands of redwood to the Alpine Lake Dam, located at 9.5 miles. Alpine Lake may look like a good place to take a dip, especially on a hot day. You will be rewarded with a stiff ticket from the Water District if you try it.

A half-mile past the lake dam begins a moderately steep section, often shaded by redwoods. You will reach the summit of this climb at 12.1 miles, at which point you will turn left onto Ridgecrest Boulevard.

Ridgecrest Boulevard will break out of the redwoods at 12.5 miles, just as you begin another moderate climb. From this point to the top of Mount Tam, you will be out in the open. There are some steep sections, and the road is generally narrow with no shoulders. The views of the Pacific, the rolling hillsides, and the looming peak of Mount Tam help to keep your mind off the climbing. At 15.9 miles, reach the intersection of Ridgecrest Boulevard and Pan Toll Road. If you intend to go all the way to the peak of Mount Tam, go straight through the intersection. Or turn right onto Pan Toll Road and start your well-deserved downhill. If there is no fog, you will get some nice views of San Francisco and the Bay Bridge.

At 19 miles, you will have reached the Mount Tamalpais East Peak, the highest peak on the mountain. There are rest rooms, water, and a kiosk with food if it is a Saturday or Sunday between 11:00 A.M. and 4:30 P.M. The elevation is 2,350 feet. If you still have not had enough

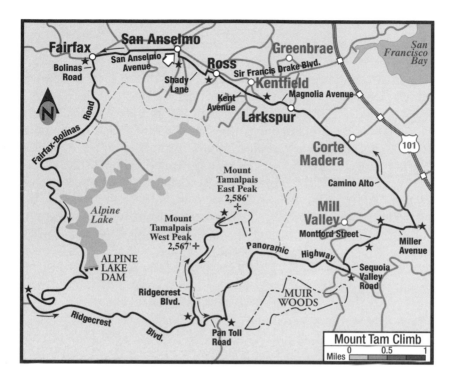

climbing, you can lock your bike and climb up to the observation building (2,571 feet in elevation).

Now you have a long descent ahead of you. Retrace your route to Pan Toll Road and turn left. This is mile 22 in your ride. Pan Toll Road ends in a T at Panoramic Highway at 23.4 miles, where you will turn left toward Mill Valley. (The Pan Toll Camp at this intersection has water and rest rooms.) The descent here is rapid, so keep things under control. The road is in good condition but can be busy, especially on summer weekends. Watch for cars swinging abruptly into your lane.

At 27.9 miles, Panoramic Highway intersects Sequoia Valley Road and Muir Woods Road. Take a sharp left onto Sequoia Valley Road. Near the city limits of Mill Valley (at approximately 28.5 miles), Sequoia becomes Edgewood Avenue. Later, Edgewood becomes Molino Avenue. Follow the Ride Guide for directions through Mill Valley. You have reached the base of Mount Tamalpais. Getting back probably did not take as long as it took to climb the mountain.

Once on Camino Alto, get set for one last 2-mile climb, starting at about mile 30.7. The gradual climb takes you to the summit at 32.7 miles, where the road becomes Corte Madera Avenue. It changes names again at 34 miles to Magnolia Avenue as you head into Larkspur. At 35.9 miles, bear left onto Kent Avenue; the market at this intersection has shaded picnic tables, cold drinks, and a good deli.

Continue on Kent, pass the College of Marin, and enter Ross at 36.4 miles. Take a left onto Lagunitas Road at 36.8 miles, then a right onto Shady Lane. Another right onto Bolinas Avenue and a left onto San Anselmo Avenue take you back to your starting point.

RIDE GUIDE

0.0 From intersection of San Anselmo Avenue and Center Boulevard, follow green and white Bike Route signs that keep you on San Anselmo Avenue.

0.3 Turn right to continue on San Anselmo Avenue.

0.9 Ride onto Landsdale Avenue.

1.1 Fairfax.

1.3 At T, turn left onto Broadway.

★ 1.6 Turn left onto Bolinas Road.

2.0 Bear left to continue on route.

2.6 Route becomes Fairfax-Bolinas Road.

4.2 Mount Tamalpais Watershed.

9.5 Alpine Lake Dam.

★ 12.1 Turn left onto Ridgecrest Boulevard.

15.9 Continue straight to top of Mount Tam.

★ 19.0 Mount Tamalpais East Peak. Turn around and return the way you came.

★ 22.0 Turn left onto Pan Toll Road.

★ 23.4 At T, turn left onto Panoramic Highway.

★ 27.9 Turn left onto Sequoia Valley Road.

28.7 Route becomes Edgewood Avenue.

29.1 Route becomes Molino Avenue.

29.5 Turn right onto James Street, following green and white Bike Route signs.

30.0 Ride onto Molino Avenue.

★ 30.1 Turn left onto Montford Street.

★ 30.2 Turn right onto Miller Avenue.

★ 30.7 Turn left onto Camino Alto.

32.7 Route becomes Corte Madera Avenue.
34.0 Route becomes Magnolia Avenue.
34.7 Ride onto bike path, which parallels Magnolia Avenue.
★ 35.9 Bear left onto Kent Avenue.
36.4 Ross.
36.8 At T, turn left onto Lagunitas Road.
★ 36.9 Turn right onto Shady Lane.
37.1 Turn right onto Bolinas Avenue.
37.5 Turn left onto San Anselmo Avenue.
38.0 End of ride.

St. Helena

Submitted by Alan Bloom

Wineries are scattered along this 51.5-mile route as it winds through the spectacular Napa Valley, the most famous wine-producing region in the United States.

Type of ride: road bike
Starting point: St. Helena
Finishing point: same
Distance: 51.5 miles round trip
Level of difficulty: moderate
General terrain: moderately hilly
Traffic conditions: light traffic
Estimated riding time (range): 3.0 to 4.5 hours
Best season/time of day to ride: weekdays
Points of interest: many wineries on route; Silverado Museum
Accommodations and services: groceries in St. Helena and Angwin (note that Angwin stores may be closed on Saturdays; see text), several campgrounds in Lake Berryessa, Bothe–Napa Valley State Park 5 miles north of St. Helena

GETTING THERE
From San Francisco, take US 101 north (over the Golden Gate Bridge), driving 28 miles to Novato. Turn right (east) onto State Route 37, and

drive 22 miles to the junction with State Route 29. Turn left (north) onto State Route 29 and travel 30 miles through Napa, Yountville, and Rutherford to St. Helena. The Safeway parking lot on Church Street is a good place to park (and to stock up on supplies for the ride).

IN THE SADDLE

North of San Francisco lie the valleys and hills synonymous with California wine country. Large and small wineries dot the countryside, with architecture ranging from nineteenth-century European to more contemporary designs. The greatest concentration of wineries flanks State Highway 29 north and south of St. Helena. A parallel road, the Silverado Trail, has additional wineries sprinkled along the slopes of the east hills.

Wine has been the economic and cultural heart of the Napa Valley since the mid-1800s. The first Europeans to arrive in the valley were from the Sonoma Mission, founded in 1823 under the leadership of Father Jose Altimira. The priests were looking initially for sheltered inland pastures for horses and cattle, but found the valley a fertile place for growing olives, figs, and a Mexican strain of grape called the Mission Grape.

The first white settler to live among the tribes of Native Americans (principally Miwok) in the Napa Valley was George Yount. In 1831 Yount was given a Mexican land grant of 11,800 acres, which comprised the heart of what is today the Napa Valley. Yount worked well with the local tribes, and together they cultivated vineyards, raised sheep and cattle, and constructed mills for flour and lumber.

At his death, Yount was honored by valley residents when they changed the name of the principal village, Sebastopol, to Yountville. His death also marked the end of the Mexican land grant era in the Napa Valley; his lands were sold off to numerous settlers who moved into the valley and maintained or started additional orchards and vineyards. The arrival of the wagon trains in the 1840s and the gold seekers in the early 1850s spurred commercial development in the area.

In the mid-1850s, Charles Krug introduced European wine-making techniques, still using the Mission Grape. Krug acquired a tract of land, built

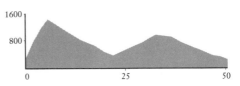

a store, and offered free lots to anyone who would settle in his town-site. The resulting community of St. Helena was platted in 1853. Many of the original inhabitants of Krug's St. Helena came from Switzerland, Germany, and Italy. They brought with them generations of knowledge about growing different varieties of grapes. The fertile valley was also suitable for fruit orchards, and groves of apricot, cherry, plum, pear, and peach trees were established.

In 1860, Count Agostin Haraszthy introduced European strains of grapes into the valley for the first time. Within a decade there were thousands of Napa Valley acres given to vineyards. The wine yield burgeoned from a total production of 8,500 gallons in the 1860s to 4 million gallons within 20 years.

The Silverado Museum in St. Helena (1490 Library Lane), with its extensive collection of Robert Louis Stevenson memorabilia, is definitely worth a visit. How did this Scottish author of *Treasure Island* and many other well-known adventure stories come to be associated with St.

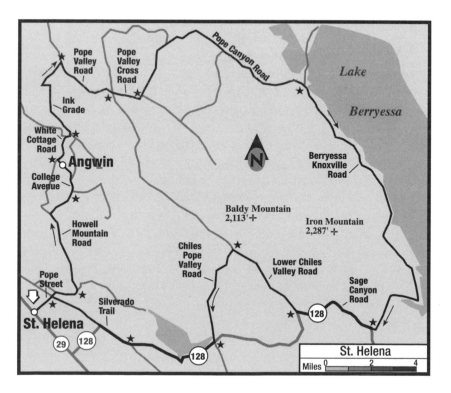

Helena? He met his American bride-to-be at an artist's colony in France and followed her home to California. One hitch before they could be hitched: Fanny was married to another. While waiting for his fiancée's divorce, Stevenson lived in Monterey, San Francisco, and Oakland. During the wait he became quite ill. In the spring of 1880 Fanny was finally free to tie the knot. Too poor to afford hotels, and with Robert too sick to travel very far, the newlyweds took their honeymoon in an abandoned bunkhouse at the Old Silverado Mine on Mount St. Helena, overlooking the Napa Valley. Almost overnight, Stevenson regained his health, and the couple returned to Scotland, where he penned his adventure masterpieces.

Next door to the Silverado Museum is the Napa Valley Wine Library. If you are looking for information on anything related to the grape—history, growing, or the making and drinking of wine —it is most likely in this collection. Both the museum and the library are open to the public (the museum is closed on Mondays and holidays).

You will have a long climb of moderate difficulty as you cycle away from St. Helena along the Howell Mountain Road. The town of Angwin that you will pass through is built around Pacific Union College, established by the Seventh Day Adventist Conference for training ministers, doctors, nurses, and teachers. The college was established in the crater of an extinct volcano. The mountain was drilled to a depth of 600 feet, where water at a temperature of 97 degrees was tapped. The top ridge of the crater (Howell Mountain) is just high enough that on a clear day you can see both San Francisco and the Sierra Nevada range.

Angwin is not your typical college town; you will not find espresso stands on every corner. In fact, you will not find coffee, tea, alcohol, or cigarettes for sale even in the downtown grocery. (Also, few services will be available on Saturday, the Seventh Day Adventist Sabbath.)

So have a cold drink, and drop down the Ink Grade into Pope Canyon. It is a pretty easy pedal to Lake Berryessa, located in the dry, grassy hills that separate the Napa Valley from the Sacramento Valley. This lake is a popular summer haunt of water-skiers and boaters. It offers good fishing year-round, with plenty of quiet, cool coves for summer anglers. Here you can try for blue gill, Kokanee salmon, trout, and bass.

You will return to St. Helena after circumnavigating Iron Mountain (2,287 feet elevation), Baldy Mountain (2,113 feet elevation), Lake Hennessey via Sage Canyon (State Highway 128), Chiles Pope Valley

Road, and the Silverado Trail. The latter is the remains of an old stage-coach route that once meandered through the Napa Valley.

RIDE GUIDE

    0.0 From the parking lot at the corner of Church Street and Pope Street in St. Helena, turn right onto Pope Street.

★   0.8 Bear left onto Howell Mountain Road.

    4.9 Turn right to continue on Howell Mountain Road.

★   6.9 Turn left onto College Avenue.

★   7.6 Turn right onto White Cottage Road.

★   8.6 Turn left onto Ink Grade.

★ 11.6 Turn right onto Pope Valley Road.

★ 13.8 Bear left onto Pope Valley Cross Road.

★ 14.8 Turn left onto Pope Canyon Road.

★ 22.9 Turn right onto Berryessa Knoxville Road.

★ 34.9 Turn right onto SR 128 (Sage Canyon Road).

★ 38.0 Turn right onto Lower Chiles Valley Road.

★ 41.1 Turn left onto Chiles Pope Valley Road.

★ 44.3 Turn right onto SR 128 (Sage Canyon Road).

★ 47.6 Turn right onto Silverado Trail.

★ 50.7 Turn left onto Pope Street.

  51.5 Turn right onto Church Street. End of ride.

22 Berkeley Loop
Submitted by Don Gray

This 43-mile loop ride takes you around the Berkeley area from the Robert Sibley Volcanic Regional Reserve to the Tilden Regional Park and back through the University of California at Berkeley.

Type of ride: road bike
Starting point: Berkeley
Finishing point: same
Distance: 43.1 miles round trip
Level of difficulty: difficult
General terrain: hilly; total elevation 4,000 feet

Traffic conditions: two-lane light traffic
Estimated riding time: 4 to 5 hours
Best season/time of day to ride: spring through fall
Points of interest: great views of San Francisco Bay, Golden Gate
    Bridge, Alcatraz
Accommodations and services: full services in Berkeley and Oakland.

GETTING THERE

This ride starts at the University of California in Berkeley. From San Francisco, take I-80 east across the bay. Exit onto US Highway 580 and drive 1 mile east to State Highway 24. Exit east onto State Highway 24. Drive approximately 2 miles and exit south onto College Avenue. Drive 2 blocks and park at the BART (Bay Area Rapid Transit) station.

IN THE SADDLE

This ride traverses several of the ridges above the communities of Berkeley and Oakland. Once you leave behind the 6 miles of suburban riding at the beginning of the ride, you will be using mostly lightly trafficked two-lane roads.

Oakland and Berkeley are framed by the relatively low (up to about 1,200 feet) Berkeley Hills, which parallel the shoreline of the bay. As you reach the top of the wooded slopes of the ridge, you will see to the east the higher elevations of the Contra Costa Hills, culminating in Mount Diablo (3,849 feet) about 30 miles east of Oakland.

Rugged Mount Diablo rises alone from a level plain to dominate the surrounding countryside. This conical, volcano-like outline can be seen for great distances in every direction, and served as a common marker for Native Americans, explorers, and pioneers. In 1851, Mount Diablo was chosen as the base point for USGS surveys in California; the positions of most of the lands in northern and central California are referenced to this single point. Mount Diablo apparently took its name from the beliefs of natives and explorers alike that the mountain was haunted by spirits (*diablo* is Spanish for devil or spirit).

At the top of your climb onto the ridge is Skyline Boulevard, which offers excellent views of the Contra

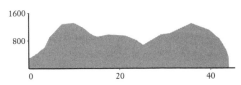

Costa Hills to the east, Alcatraz Prison, and the jagged silhouette of San Francisco.

Your route will take you through a number of large and small parks and forest preserves. At the end of your climb up the ridge is the Robert Sibley Volcanic Regional Preserve, sitting on the remnants of what was once the East Bay's dominant volcano. There is a self-guided trail over Round Top Peak, a favorite of amateur and professional geologists interested in the origins of the Bay Area.

One of the first parks you will reach is the Joaquin Miller Park, named for the poet who once attempted to form an artist's colony on his 80-acre homestead. If you detour onto Joaquin Miller Road, in 0.3 mile you will come to a ranger station that houses a small display about Joaquin Miller. The writer's works are largely ignored today, but he left a lasting legacy in the redwoods he planted on his property. This park is considered the world's only urban redwood forest.

As you turn onto Redwood Road you will follow the southern perimeter of the beautiful 2,000-acre Redwood Regional Park. For enjoyable mountain bike rides within this park, you can obtain a free map at one of the park's several entrances. A more detailed map, The Rambler's Guide to the Trails of the East Bay Hills, is available through the Olmsted Brothers Map Company, P.O. Box 5351, Berkeley, CA 94705; phone (510) 658-4869.

The Redwood Park straddles two north–south ridges. As you enter the park you will descend the west ridge and then climb the east ridge. As you turn onto Pinehurst Road, you can look down into the San Leandro Reservoir. Much of this area was logged in the early 1850s when the Patten brothers gave up their search for gold and instead leased sections of the Peralta Redwoods, a stand of giant trees that once extended from the top of the ridge midway to the Oakland estuary. More than 400 men were employed in the Patten operations, cutting lumber for the building of San Francisco, Oakland, and Berkeley. Today the area is covered with second- and even third-growth trees.

Moraga Way and Wildcat Canyon Road will take you along the east ridge north toward the San Pablo Reservoir. Wildcat Canyon Road will take you into Tilden Regional Park. If you are interested in botany, the Regional Parks Botanic Garden is located at the junction of Wildcat Canyon Road and South Park Drive. At this junction you can also shorten the ride by using South Park Drive, which traverses the edge

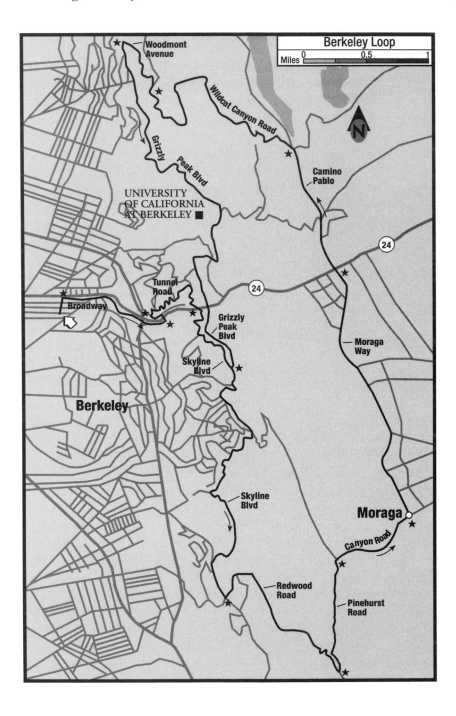

of a large golf course, to intersect Grizzly Peak Boulevard to the south. Grizzly Peak Boulevard will take you back to Skyline Boulevard for your return to Berkeley.

The ridges here were once part of the 46,800-acre Rancho San Antonio, granted to the Peralta family in 1820 by the Spanish Governor de Sola. For twenty years, Rancho San Antonio played an important part in the commercial and social life of the Bay Area. The American victory over Mexico in 1849 ended the era of the Spanish landowner in California; the discovery of gold at Sutter's Mill the same year only hastened the end of the era. Some would-be miners who reached the Bay Area abandoned their search for gold and instead squatted on the Peralta lands. Other settlers took a more ethical approach, choosing to lease lands from the Peralta family for farming, ranching, and lumber operations.

In 1853, title to what is now the core of Berkeley was purchased by American speculators for $82,000. The first American building in Berkeley was a roadhouse erected in 1853 near San Pablo Avenue and Delaware Streets. Oakland was incorporated by eastern financier Horace Carpentier, who populated a townsite with a handful of squatters, then installed himself in the mayor's chair. Carpentier named the town after the numerous stands of encinas (evergreen oaks) that dotted the alluvial plain.

Berkeley's real growth got started when the university was chartered in 1868 on a plain of oaks cut through by Strawberry Canyon. Eighteen months later, ten faculty were ready to begin instructing forty students. By the early 1900s Berkeley was already serving as a popular bedroom community for San Francisco commuters. Following the San Francisco earthquake and fire in 1906, the populations of Berkeley and Oakland mushroomed as San Francisco residents sought nearby accommodations while the ruined city was being rebuilt. In the fall of 1923, it was Berkeley's turn for disaster when a fire fanned by strong winds destroyed most of the city north of the campus.

As you turn off Wildcat Canyon Road and onto Woodmont Avenue and then Grizzly Peak Boulevard, you will pass above several of the better-known campus buildings, including the Lawrence Hall of Science. At the top of the ridge are wonderful views of the 1,230-acre campus and the imposing Sather Tower, still known as the Campanile. The tower houses 61 carillon bells that are played weekdays at 8 A.M., noon, and 6 P.M. On a still day the bells can be heard from the top of the ridge. If you want to spend more time exploring the campus before or after your ride, there is a visitor information center at the Student Union Building.

RIDE GUIDE

     0.0 From the BART station on College Avenue, ride north on College Avenue.

★   0.1 Turn right onto Broadway.

★   1.8 Turn left and ride under SR 24.

     1.9 Turn left onto Caldecott Lane.

★   2.1 Turn right onto Tunnel Road.

★   3.6 Ride under SR 24. Route becomes Skyline Boulevard.

★ 10.5 Turn left onto Redwood Road.

★ 13.1 Turn left onto Pinehurst Road.

★ 16.2 Turn right onto Canyon Road.

★ 18.1 Turn left onto Moraga Way.

★ 22.9 Ride under SR 24. Route becomes Camino Pablo.

★ 25.2 Bear left onto Wildcat Canyon Road.

★ 30.7 Turn left onto Woodmont Avenue.

★ 30.8 Turn left onto Grizzly Peak Boulevard.

★ 38.1 Turn right onto Skyline Boulevard.

★ 39.6 Ride under SR 24. Route becomes Tunnel Road.

★ 41.0 Turn left onto Caldecott Lane.

    41.2 Turn right and ride under SR 24.

★ 41.3 Turn right onto Broadway.

★ 43.1 Turn left onto College Avenue

    43.2 End of ride.

Region 4

Yosemite Area

View of Half Dome from the forest floor (photo by Stan Hansen)

23 American River Ride
Submitted by Nan Baker

The route takes you between the Fish Hatchery at Nimbus to Discovery Park on the edge of Sacramento along what may be the nation's oldest bike path.

Type of ride: road bike
Starting point: Nimbus Fish Hatchery
Finishing point: Discovery Park in Sacramento
Distance: 23 miles one way
Level of difficulty: easy
General terrain: flat
Traffic conditions: none
Estimated riding time: 2 to 3 hours; longer for round-trip
Best season/time of day to ride: spring through fall; summer mornings particularly nice
Points of interest: fish hatchery, American River
Accommodations and services: in nearby Sacramento

A shade-covered trail (photo by Nan Baker)

GETTING THERE

For the eastern trailhead, take the US Highway 50 Hazel off-ramp, then follow Hazel north to Nimbus Road East. Each trailhead has a parking lot with a $4 fee. If you want to start at the western trailhead (Discovery Park), exit I-5 (State Highway 99) at Garden Highway and go east to Discovery Park Road South.

Note: This trail is not suitable for fast riding. There are some narrow sections, and the trail is used by pedestrians and joggers as well as cyclists of all abilities. (Horses are also allowed on the trail between their offshoot dirt trails.) Please observe the 15-mile-per-hour speed limit.

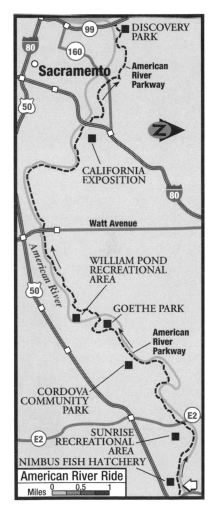

IN THE SADDLE

This is an easy 23-mile ride one way (or 46-mile round-trip) on either road or mountain bikes along the flat Jedediah Smith National Recreation Trail. Your route meanders along the American River. The well-maintained blacktop is fine for the novice or family rider, but more experienced riders will enjoy the scenery and attractions as well.

The American River Trail has quite a lengthy cycling history. According to John Elgart in *The History of the Lower American River,* the Capital City Wheelmen voted in March 1896 to construct a cinder path between the current site of Sacramento State and the town of Folsom. With the assistance of donations from club members and merchants in Sacramento and Folsom, the trail was completed

The old territorial capitol in Sacramento (photo by Gary MacFadden)

and officially designated the C. C. Wheelmen Bikeway. This makes the American River Trail one of the oldest, if not the oldest, bikeways in the United States.

Your ride starts at the eastern trailhead, the Nimbus Fish Hatchery, but the route can be easily navigated in either direction. Leaving the fish hatchery, the trail immediately winds back into trees and away from civilization. You will get many views of the American River, the waterway that started the California Gold Rush of 1849.

Captain John Sutter, a pioneer settler, had been attracted to the region by its flat stretches of unclaimed land and the navigable Sacramento and American Rivers. He founded New Helvetia (Sacramento), built a fort (much of it acquired from the Russians when they abandoned Fort Ross on the coast), herded animals, traded furs, and lived like a king.

In January 1848, Sutter's chief carpenter, James Marshall, discovered several flakes of golden metal in the tailrace of Sutter's Mill. (It is disputed that this was the first gold find in California; some historians claim Marshall's find was the second or even third.)

The rush was on. Sutter surprisingly did not fare well from the discovery at his mill. The fort and surrounding areas were quickly overrun by gold seekers, his cattle were stolen, and his rights to the lands came under dispute. He finally gave up on the region, moved to Pennsylvania, and died nearly a pauper in 1880 while still trying to regain title to his lands through congressional intervention. It is likely that Sutter would have preferred that the American River had kept its secret.

The trail passes through several parks along the way, and each has picnic tables, rest rooms, and water available. Grapes and wild berries grow along the route, and you will often see groups of people gathering them by the sackful.

Smooth trail ahead (photo by Nan Baker)

You will cycle through dense forest shade and open meadows. At the south end of Goethe Park, the trail crosses a long bridge, with places to pull over and view the river. Eventually, signs of civilization begin to show up, including high tension wires and a well-manicured golf course. Discovery Park will appear out of the trees; it is a wonderful place to stop for lunch or a nap in the shade. Just stay on the east end of the park, away from the freeway.

You can arrange to be picked up or turn around and pedal back to the Nimbus Fish Hatchery to retrieve your vehicle. Allow between 2 and 3 hours in each direction. Remember to keep your speed down to the posted 15 miles per hour.

RIDE GUIDE
    0.0 From Nimbus Fish Hatchery, ride west on American River
        Parkway.
    2.5 Sunrise Recreational Area.
    7.1 Cordova Community Park.
    8.6 William Pond Recreational Area.
  10.6 Rio Americano High School.
  16.0 California Exposition.
  22.5 Discovery Park. End of ride.

Sutter Creek

Submitted by Al Schoenemann

This hilly but low-trafficked ride takes you into the heart of the 1849 Gold Rush country. You will get a workout early in the ride on the way to Daffodil Hill, but the return trip through Volcano and back to Sutter Creek is all downhill.

Type of ride: road bike
Starting point: Sutter Creek
Finishing point: same
Distance: 34.4 miles
Level of difficulty: moderate
General terrain: hilly, with three creek crossings; 7 miles of gravel
Traffic conditions: light traffic on narrow two-lane roads with minimal shoulders
Estimated riding time: 5 to 7 hours
Best season/time of day to ride: March through May best months, when the Sierra foothills are green and the wildflowers are in bloom
Points of interest: gold-rush-era towns, scenic rural roads
Accommodations and services: all services except for a bike shop

GETTING THERE

Follow State Highway 16 east out of Sacramento for 20 miles to the junction with State Highway 49. Go south on State Highway 49 for 6 miles to Sutter Creek. Park in the public parking lot on Main Street (State Highway 49) on the south end of Sutter Creek.

IN THE SADDLE

Sutter Creek was a town founded by miners who decided to stay in the area after the first wave of gold fever had died down. There were some sizable strikes made in this area as well. The mining business was expensive here: Shafts had to be bored through solid rock, timbers were erected to prevent cave-ins, equipment was shipped long distances from the east, and the ore

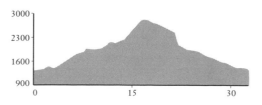

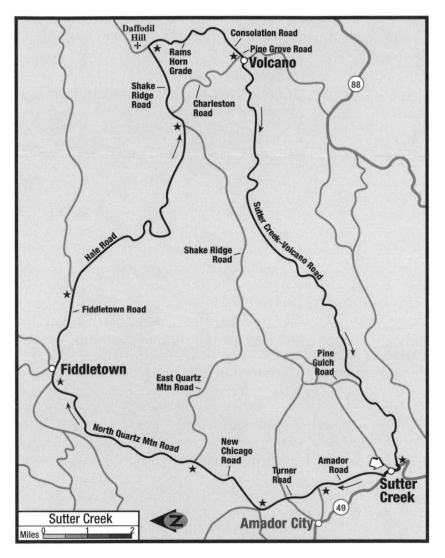

was shipped out for processing. Leland Stanford, who poured thousands of dollars into his Lincoln Mine, once offered to sell it for $5,000. He persevered and in the end made a fortune from the mine and then sold it for $400,000. This money backed his development of the Central Pacific Railroad, which in turn produced a large portion of the millions that later endowed Stanford University.

Head north out of Sutter Creek on Main Street (State Highway 49).

Turn right onto Amador Road and follow it to the junction with Amador Creek Road. Here, Amador Road becomes Turner Road. Continue north on Turner Road to New Chicago Road. Bear right onto New Chicago Road and follow it to the junction with North Quartz Mountain Road. Through this section you should experience very light traffic, which will help to take your mind off the climbing. Several portions of the loop follow creeks, which afford some level sections of riding.

Continue north on North Quartz Mountain Road. (East Quartz Mountain and Shake Ridge Roads can be used to form a shorter loop into Volcano.)

Continue on North Quartz Mountain Road until the junction with Fiddletown Road. Fiddletown was settled in 1849 by a group of gold seekers from Missouri. According to legend, because the Missourians were always fiddling, the place became known as Fiddletown. In 1878, a judge who was embarrassed at being known as "the judge from Fiddletown" had the town's name officially changed to Oleta, but that did not last for long, and the original name was revived. Bret Harte, the frontier writer, even used the town's name in the title of his story "An Episode of Fiddletown."

Turn right onto Fiddletown Road and ride for approximately 3 miles along Dry Creek to the junction with Hale Road. Turn right onto Hale Road and follow it to the junction with Shake Ridge Road; then turn left. Pass an astronomical observatory as you approach Daffodil Hill and the junction with Rams Horn Grade. Turn right onto Rams Horn Grade and follow it to the town of Volcano.

It is hard to believe when looking at it today that Volcano—named for the craterlike hollow in which the town resides—was once one of the richest and most populous towns of the Mother Lode. Rich deposits were found in nearby Soldiers Gulch in 1849; by 1850, the town boasted saloons, a Masonic Hall, and an express shipping building.

Leaving Volcano, take the Sutter Creek–Volcano Road. This road usually carries light traffic, except in the spring when the daffodils are blooming. Then dozens of people drive to view the flowers and picnic at Daffodil Hill, where there is a small resort area. Remain on Sutter Creek–Volcano Road, enjoying the downhill, all the way back to Sutter Creek and the end of the ride.

RIDE GUIDE

    0.0 From public parking lot on Main Street (SR 49) at south end of Sutter Creek, ride north on Main Street.

    0.5 Turn right onto Amador Creek Street.

★ 1.8 Route becomes Turner Road.

★ 3.1 Route becomes New Chicago Road.

★ 4.6 Turn left onto North Quartz Mountain Road.

★ 8.7 Turn right onto Fiddletown Road.

    9.0 Fiddletown.

★ 12.1 Turn right onto Hale Road.

★ 17.2 Turn left onto Shake Ridge Road.

★ 21.1 Turn right onto Rams Horn Grade.

  21.9 Ride onto Consolation Road.

★ 22.1 Turn left onto Pine Grove Road. Volcano.

★ 23.2 Turn right onto Sutter Creek–Volcano Road.

  33.4 Ride onto Church Street.

★ 33.5 Turn right onto SR 49.

  34.4 End of ride.

Oakdale to Yosemite

Submitted by Stan Hansen

This ride up the Stanislaus River Valley and Sierra Nevada foothills takes you to the breathtaking vistas of one of this country's premier National Park treasures: Yosemite.

Type of ride: road bike
Starting point: Oakdale
Finishing point: Yosemite Village, Yosemite National Park
Distance: 100 miles
Level of difficulty: moderate
General terrain: mountainous
Traffic conditions: vary; light on much of the early ride, heavier near the park
Estimated riding time: 2 days

Best season/time of day to ride: weekdays in May and June or September and October

Points of interest: scenic views in the Stanislaus River, La Grange, and Yosemite Valleys; historic gold-mining towns

Accommodations and services: some hotels and campgrounds along route and at Yosemite National Park

Supplemental maps or other information: AAA maps; park guide available at Yosemite National Park entrance

GETTING THERE

From Sacramento, head south on Interstate 99 past Stockton. As you approach Menteca, take the Yosemite Avenue (State Highway 120) exit and head east. After about 15 miles, look for the River Road–Rodden Road intersection (with a traffic light) just before you enter downtown Oakdale. From Los Angeles, head north on Interstate 5; past the Grapevine Grade, take State Highway 99 north past Bakersfield and Fresno. As you enter Turlock, take the Lander Avenue exit and head north through downtown Turlock, staying north on Geer Road (State Highway J14) past State Highway 132 to Oakdale. Stay north on State Highway 120 past downtown Oakdale to the River Road–Rodden Road intersection. Park near the traffic light.

IN THE SADDLE

This route has a fair amount of climbing from Oakdale to Yosemite National Park, but it is scaled about right for a 2-day self-contained tour. Some hardy souls have proven that you can accomplish the 100-mile ride in a single day, but you will miss a lot of enjoyment and scenery with this approach. Note that a weekday in May, June, September, or October is highly recommended due to the levels of automobile traffic Yosemite Park draws on the weekends in the high season.

Start traveling east on Rodden Road through the Stanislaus River Valley. Watch for a private home called The Castle (complete with draw-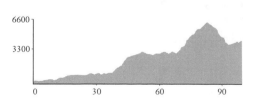bridge) and a beautiful walnut grove lining the road. At 6.6 miles, Rodden Road ends where Orange Blossom Road comes over the two-lane bridge and follows the north bank of the river. Continue on Orange Blossom Road through open meadows and small ranches.

At 10.6 miles, turn right onto Morrison Road and begin a 2-mile climb out of the river valley. At the summit of this climb, Morrison Road becomes Cemetery Road. Begin a steep descent into the gold-rush supply town of Knights Ferry. Turn right onto Sonora Road and bear left as Sonora Road becomes Main Street through Knights Ferry. The general store—established in 1852 and recognized as the oldest continuously operating store in the state—makes a good place for a rest and snacks. Also on Main Street are the Knights Ferry Visitor Center and Historical Park. Near the visitor center is a hiker/biker gate; go through it and ride past the ruins of an old mill and other buildings and arrive at a covered bridge crossing the Stanislaus River. This is the longest wood-covered bridge on the West Coast. About 20 years ago, it stopped carrying automobile traffic, so pedestrians and cyclists now have it to themselves. Through the occasional windows you can catch glimpses of the river and its rocky shoreline. After the bridge, head straight onto what is now Shuper Road, through another hiker/biker gate and climb the short grade up to Sonora Road. Turn left onto Sonora for a short distance and then left again onto Yosemite Highway (State Highway 120).

The Yosemite Highway often carries a high amount of traffic, but the 6- to 8-foot shoulders give you plenty of room. Begin a stiff climb (from 200 feet to 1,400 feet) that lasts for the next 5 miles. Midday shade

Covered bridge at Knights Ferry (photo by Stan Hansen)

is scarce on this section, so take your time—along with plenty of water bottles. At the top of the grade, you will have a nice coast down into the La Grange Valley and about 8 miles of rolling hills through some nice scenery. At 23.7 miles, pass the La Grange Road cutoff, which would take you to the town of La Grange 17 miles to the south. You want to continue on Yosemite Highway (State Highway 120).

At 27.6 miles, you will come to Yosemite Junction. Take the turn to the right. There is a market here with water, food, and other refreshments. State Highway 120 is joined by State Highway 49 as they follow the same route toward Chinese Camp and Moccasin. The shoulder narrows to 2 to 3 feet, and you will have a few short climbing pitches as you head toward Chinese Camp, at 31.5 miles. This small town was founded in 1849 for the Chinese miners. It was also a stagecoach stop in the 1850s. There are several markets available. A nice descent will

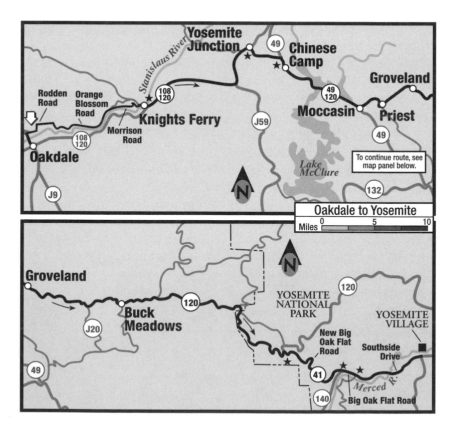

take you to the shore of the Don Pedro Reservoir, a human-made lake that stores water from the Tuolumne River. Follow the reservoir's shoreline for about 5 miles to the town of Moccasin.

This town is unique in that it is owned and operated by the city and county of San Francisco. Here, water from the Hetch Hetchey Reservoir descends through several large pipes, driving a hydroelectric generator and then continuing toward San Francisco. There is a general store here and some nice shade trees where you can contemplate your next challenge: the Big Oak Flat Grade.

This will be your major climb of this day's ride. The Big Oak Flat Grade consists of a maze of switchbacks climbing 2,000 feet in 4.5 miles. In a low gear, this will take you between 45 and 60 minutes. A cafe at the 2,000-foot elevation marker is the only service between Moccasin and the Priest Resort near the top of the grade (at mile 46). Make sure you have plenty of water. You may be tempted to use an alternate road, Priest Grade Road, which climbs 2,000 feet in only 2 miles. It is not recommended unless you enjoy pushing your bike.

At Priest, you will get a commanding view of the Don Pedro Reservoir and the La Grange Valley. You have a half mile of steep pitch left to the town of Big Oak Flat and some less intense climbing after the town, but the worst is over. A swift 1.5-mile downhill takes you into Groveland, approximately the halfway point in the tour. There are a number of cafes and markets to choose from and a nice town park where you can stop and rest. There are several accommodations for indoor overnights or you can camp at Yosemite Pines, which is approximately 2 miles southeast of Groveland on State Highway 120 (Old Highway Road).

If you do camp overnight, backtrack into Groveland in the morning and pick up Ferretti Road just past the market at the east end of Groveland. You could continue on State Highway 120, but the traffic is much higher there and features several long, hard climbs. On Ferretti Road, you will loop around the Pine Mountain recreation area and cruise through several beautiful pine groves. Ferretti Road will lead you back to State Highway 120 at the 59-mile point in your ride, where you will find a nice little cafe for a possible breakfast stop. Turn left onto State Highway 120 for some more climbing.

Pass the Groveland Ranger Station and come into Buck Meadows at mile 62.5. Here is the last cafe along the route until you enter Yosemite National Park.

From here on, allow time at pullouts such as the Rim of the World vista point (mile 64). You have done some major climbing on this ride, so you deserve the sightseeing time. After crossing a bridge spanning the Tuolumne River, you will face a climb that is seemingly endless, but in reality it is only 4 miles in length. The climbing is interspersed with brief but enjoyable downhills. At Yosemite Lakes turnoff (mile 70.5) is a small market. This is the last grocery stop until you reach Yosemite Valley and a good place to replenish your water supply.

At just over the 75-mile point, enter Yosemite National Park, at an elevation of 4,892 feet. Bicyclists pay a $3 entrance fee, which entitles them to 7 days in the park. There are rest rooms and water available.

There are still several steep climbs ahead before you reach the peak elevation in the ride at Crane Flat (6,142 feet) at 83.4 miles. (There is a hiker/biker campground at Crane Flat.) Pass the Merced Grove of Giant Sequoias at 80.5 miles and the Tuolumne Groves at 83.8. The thick forest will begin to open with views of the Yosemite Valley. If you are an Ansel Adams fan, things should quickly start looking familiar.

At approximately 84 miles, you will reach the junction of State Highway 120 and New Big Oak Flat Road. Turn right onto New Big Oak Flat Road (State Highway 120 continues northeast over Tioga Pass). What follows is a wonderful 10-mile descent into the Yosemite Valley which you could probably do in 20 minutes if you spare the brakes, but we recommend you take it slowly and enjoy the scenery.

At 90.5 miles, you will go through a 0.25-mile-long tunnel and pass a series of waterfalls and cascades. At the junction of Big Oak Flat Road and State Highway 140, turn left to proceed to the central area of the Yosemite Valley. At Valley View junction, turn right and cross the Merced River and Bridalveil Meadow. You will join Southside Drive. Watch the shoulder area here; in places it is quite broken.

Just past the Yosemite Chapel, you can cross Sentinel Bridge to enter Yosemite Village. Your trip odometer should roll over to 100 miles as you enter Yosemite Village. You have reached a splendid destination. Campgrounds are available nearby, as are indoor lodgings. Plan to stay in Yosemite long enough to appreciate this magnificent park.

RIDE GUIDE

0.0 From Oakdale, ride east on Rodden Road.

0.7 Turn right to continue on Rodden Road.

1.7 Turn right to continue on Rodden Road.

6.6 Ride straight onto Orange Blossom Road.

10.6 Turn right onto Morrison Road.

11.1 Ride straight onto Cemetery Road.

12.4 Knights Ferry.

13.1 Turn right onto Sonora Road which turns into Main Street.

13.9 Turn left onto Kennedy Road.

★ 14.3 Turn left onto SR 120/108.

★ 27.6 Turn right at Yosemite Junction to continue on SR 120.

★ 30.2 Bear right to continue on SR 120. SR 49 joins route.

31.5 Chinese Camp.

45.9 Priest.

49.2 Groveland.

62.5 Buck Meadows.

75.2 Big Oak Flat entrance to Yosemite National Park.

★ 83.8 Turn right onto SR 41 (New Big Oak Flat Road).

★ 93.1 Turn left to continue on SR 41 (Big Oak Flat Road). SR 140 joins route.

95.8 At Valley Junction, turn right and cross Merced River.

★ 96.1 Bear left onto Southside Drive.

100.2 Yosemite Village. End of ride.

26 Eldorado Climb
Submitted by William Paxson

This 50-mile road bike ride through the mountains of the Eldorado National Forest is designed especially for those who like to do some climbing and then coast back to where they are spending the night. You should allow 4 to 6 hours, depending upon how strong a climber you are. Given the combination of climbing, altitude gain, and fast descent, both the bicycle and the cyclist should be in good condition.

Type of ride: road bike
Starting point: Pollock Pines
Finishing point: same
Distance: 50 miles

Level of difficulty: hard

General terrain: hilly

Traffic conditions: very light on two-lane roads with wide shoulders for the majority of the route

Estimated riding time: 4 hours or more depending upon how strong a climber you are

Best season/time of day to ride: late June through mid-September

Points of interest: most of the route used by wagon trains 100 to 150 years ago; views of Sierra Nevada Peaks and Desolation Valley Wilderness

Accommodations and services: all services except bike service in nearby communities

Supplemental maps or other information: available from Eldorado Information Center, 3070 Camino Heights Drive, Camino, CA 95709; (916) 644-6048

GETTING THERE

The Eldorado Climb begins near Pollock Pines. Pollock Pines is on US Highway 50, 1 hour east of Sacramento and 1 hour southwest of South Lake Tahoe. At Pollock Pines, take the Sly Park off-ramp and look for a sign that will tell you if the Mormon Emigrant Trail is open. Because of snow, this route is normally rideable only between late June and mid-September, although some years it is open earlier in June. On maps other than the one in this book, the road is variously called Mormon Emigrant Trail, Iron Mountain Road, and—on some older maps—the Silver Lake Road.

From Pollock Pines, follow the signs to Sly Park. On Sly Park Road (County Road E16), proceed south approximately 5 miles. Go past Sly Park (a public campground) on your left, then Jenkinson Lake, again on your left. At the south end of Jenkinson Lake, turn left (east) onto the Mormon Emigrant Trail. Cross a small dam, drive through a wooded area, come to another small dam, and park anywhere off the pavement. From here the bike route proceeds east.

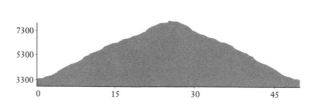

IN THE SADDLE

There are no services along the route, so you will have to go completely self-contained. Carry plenty of water and snacks. Maps show creeks and springs near the road in places, but these are not easily accessible. Moreover, water from them should be treated before you drink it.

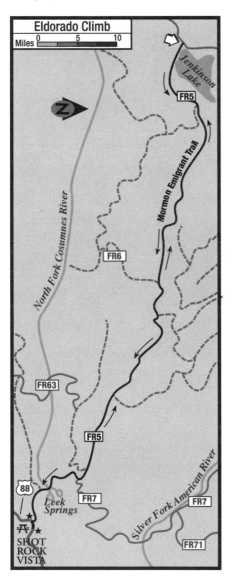

This is an out-and-back, uphill-downhill ride. The out portion of the route is uphill, so anytime you get tired of climbing you can turn around and coast back to your car or campsite. The elevation at the start of the ride is 3,500 feet. At the highest point (the turnaround) you will be riding at 7,600 feet. Most of the grades are long but not particularly steep.

As you follow the Mormon Emigrant Trail, you will be tracing a route the pioneers traveled a century and a half ago. Where the pioneers ate trail dust raised by oxen and wagons, you will be skimming along on smooth pavement through one of the nicest stretches of the Eldorado National Forest. The road is wide, the traffic is generally light, and the visibility is good.

You will be riding through a seemingly endless stretch of pine and fir trees. When there is an opening in the trees, you will be treated to breathtaking views of the high Sierra.

In July 1848, a group of

Shot Rock Vista (photo by William Paxson)

Mormons passed here on their way from Sutter's Fort (now Sacramento) to Salt Lake City. They trekked eastward on Iron Mountain Ridge, thus opening a route that is now generally followed by the paved road you are riding. In the years after the Mormons reached Salt Lake City, thousands of westward-bound gold seekers and settlers came to California, tracing backwards this route carved by the Mormon pioneers. It thus became known as the Mormon Emigrant Trail. You will pass a number of historical information markers that will give you a good reason to take a rest from your climbing.

At the 8-mile point to your left, you will begin to see views of Desolation Wilderness and the mountains just west of Lake Tahoe. This Sierra Nevada scenery will be with you off and on for the rest of the ride.

At the 21.6-mile mark, enter the top end of Leek Springs Valley. Pioneers named the spring they found here after the abundant wild leeks (a pungent garden herb that resembles an onion in taste) that grew in the area. The springs form the headwaters of the North Fork of the Cosumnes River.

Three miles farther turn right into Shot Rock Vista, which is the turnaround point for the ride. Shot Rock offers a great view, picnic tables, and pit toilets but no water.

When it is time to retrace your route back to Sly Park, turn left onto State Highway 88 and watch for the sign marking the Mormon Emigrant Trail. You will be descending quickly, and the turnoff is a sharp right turn that comes up quickly. Remember to use caution on the downhill run back to the dam (or the Sly Park Campground, if you are staying overnight).

To soak up a little more history and tackle some more climbing, turn right out of Shot Rock and ride on State Highway 88 another 4 miles. Visit the scenic and historical points of Maiden's Grave, Devil's Garden, and Tragedy Springs. If you go any farther than Tragedy Springs, you will be descending to Silver Lake and you will face a strenuous 2-mile climb on your return.

RIDE GUIDE

    0.0 From Jenkinson Lake and Sly Park, ride east on the Mormon Emigrant Trail.

  23.8 Trails West historical marker on left.

★ 23.9 Turn right onto SR 88.

★ 24.6 Turn left into Shot Rock Vista.

  24.7 Shot Rock Vista. Turnaround point.

★ 24.8 Turn left onto SR 88.

★ 25.5 Turn right onto the Mormon Emigrant Trail.

  49.4 Jenkinson Lake. End of ride.

Knights Ferry

27

Submitted by Jean O'Brien

This is an easy, 40-mile ride over gently rolling hills, suitable for either families or novice riders.

Type of ride: road bike
Starting point: Knights Ferry
Finishing point: same
Distance: 40 miles
Level of difficulty: easy
General terrain: flat to moderately rolling
Traffic conditions: light traffic
Estimated riding time: 3.5 hours
Best season/time of day to ride: spring and fall
Points of interest: covered bridge at Knights Ferry
Accommodations and services: all services in Knights Ferry and nearby Modesto

GETTING THERE

The ride begins and ends in the small community of Knights Ferry, northeast of Modesto, just off State Highway 108. The starting point for the route is the parking lot at the Knights Ferry Recreation Area in Knights Ferry. The park opens at 6:00 A.M. daily; the information office is closed on weekends, but the rest rooms are always open and rangers are usually available for information.

IN THE SADDLE

Before or after your ride, be sure to experience cycling through the covered bridge at the park. At 330 feet in length, the Knights Ferry bridge is the longest covered bridge west of the Mississippi. It was first opened in 1863 and was reportedly designed by General Ulysses S. Grant while on a visit to Knights Ferry in 1854. The bridge and an old grist mill are several hundred feet from the parking lot.

Leave Knights Ferry on Sonora Road, after passing several historic buildings, including the Hook and Ladder Building that dates from the gold-rush days. A turn onto Orange Blossom Road will take you along the banks of the Stanislaus River toward Oakdale. The route

Stelck Ranch Windmill (photo by Jean O'Brien)

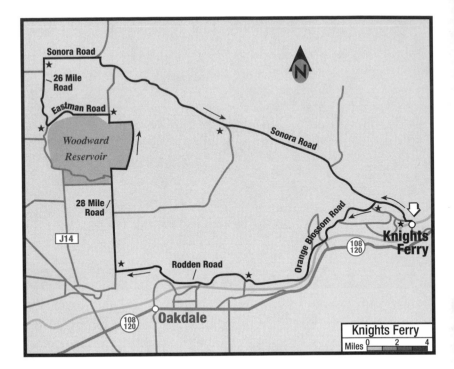

winds through horse and cattle ranches as well as orchards.

At about the 7-mile point, turn right onto Rodden Road, which will take you past walnut orchards and several houses with some interesting architecture as it skirts Oakdale, an early dairying center founded in 1871. The town is set on a plateau overlooking the Stanislaus River. Oakdale is today the home of the western factory of a well-known producer of chocolate. There are factory tours on the weekdays but not on the weekends.

Once you have turned north onto 28 Mile Road, you will have the broad and generally flat San Joaquin Valley to your left and the foothills of the Sierra gold fields on your right. At the 14-mile point, you will see the Woodward Reservoir; the route follows the east and north boundaries of this recreation area using the 28 Mile Road and Eastman Road.

The 26 Mile Road will take you north of the reservoir to rejoin Sonora Road for the return leg to Knights Ferry. At about the 23.5-mile point, just prior to the junction of 26 Mile Road and Sonora Road, watch for an old cemetery on the left. There are many graves of pioneers who came into this region. The gate is usually unlocked; please use discretion in visiting the site.

Just after the turn onto Sonora Road, cross a small bridge and pass Rosedale School, which is today a private residence. When blooming, the roses can lend a special fragrance to your ride.

Follow Sonora Road for another 10 miles, past large cattle and horse ranches, with the distant Sierra foothills as a backdrop. You will also cross several water flumes. This region was the site of some of the state's earliest water projects, storing and transporting water for irrigation and industrial purposes.

At the end of your ride, you can relax at the parking area where there are picnic tables and barbecue grills. Do not forget to visit the bridge and the historic buildings of Knights Ferry.

Miniature donkey at a horse ranch (photo by Jean O'Brien)

RIDE GUIDE

    0.0 From lower parking lot at Knights Ferry Recreation Area, turn left onto unnamed road and ride through Knights Ferry.

★ 1.2 Ride straight onto Sonora Road.

★ 1.6 Turn left onto Orange Blossom Road.

★ 7.0 Turn right onto Rodden Road.

★ 12.0 Turn right onto 28 Mile Road.

★ 18.1 Turn left onto Eastman Road.

★ 20.5 Turn right onto 26 Mile Road.

★ 25.3 Turn right onto Sonora Road.

★ 36.5 Bear left to continue on Sonora Road.

   40.1 Knights Ferry. End of ride.

A general store/insurance company from the past (photo by Jean O'Brien)

28 Ione Loop
Submitted by Al Shoenemann

This hilly route takes you on 34 miles of lightly traveled roads into the heart of the Mother Lode.

Type of ride: road bike
Starting point: Ione
Finishing point: same
Distance: 33.7 miles round trip
Level of difficulty: moderate
General terrain: hilly
Traffic conditions: two-lane roads with light traffic
Estimated riding time: 2 to 3 hours
Best season/time of day to ride: spring through fall
Points of interest: Amador County Museum in Jackson, historic reform school building in Ione, mining equipment in several towns along the route
Accommodations and services: services in Sutter Creek, Buena Vista, and Ione.

GETTING THERE
Follow State Highway 16 east out of Sacramento for 20 miles to the junction with State Highway 124. Drive south on State Highway 124 for 9 miles to Ione. Park at Howard Park, 0.5 mile south of Main Street on State Highway 124.

IN THE SADDLE
This is a hilly route through the scenic foothills of the Mother Lode country. You will begin and end your ride in Ione, which in the past has gone under the names Freeze Out and Bedbug. Once churches, homes, schools, and stores outnumbered miners' tents, the citizens decided that such frivolous names would not be fitting over, for example, the door of the new post office. The newest name honors one of the female characters in Edward Bulwer-Lytton's *The Last Days of Pompeii.*

As you depart Ione, you will see

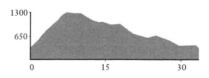

a foreboding old building on the outskirts of town that once housed the state's first reform school, the Preston School of Industry. It is now a historic monument, but it is also condemned, so there are no tours available. Some notables came out of the Preston School—including country-western singer Merle Haggard and tennis player Pancho Gonzales—proving that bad boys can make good.

The Plymouth Highway (State Route 124) and the Sutter Ione Road will lead you over the rolling terrain to Sutter Creek. In 1847, General John Augustus Sutter, in search of a site for his new sawmill, passed through what is now Sutter Creek. He later chose to locate his new mill in Coloma, near the present site of Sacramento. Had Sutter chosen instead to build his mill at Sutter Creek, the '49 gold rush might not have occurred. History tells us that Sutter's construction foreman discovered gold in the Coloma sawmill's tail race, and this discovery led directly to the gold rush. Sutter did establish a lumber camp at Sutter Creek, and

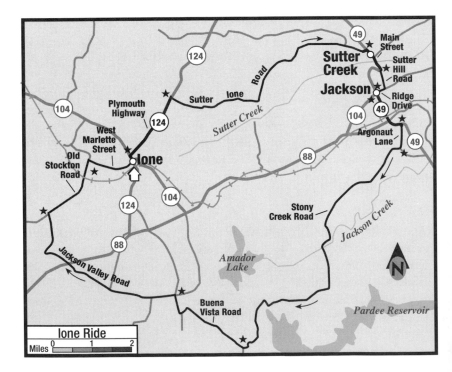

so the town bears his name. Gold—and plenty of it—was eventually discovered here, and the town grew around the Central Eureka Mine and other hard rock quartz mines.

From Sutter Creek you will follow Sutter Hill Road and Ridge Drive into Jackson. This community grew up as a rambunctious little stop-over on the Sacramento–Stockton branch of the old Carson Pass Emigrant Trail. The town desired some political status, and when they could not achieve it through the electoral process, Jackson's citizens literally stole the county seat. With plenty of gold in their pouches, the Jackson city fathers traveled to nearby Double Springs, then the county seat, and invited all the county officers to refreshments at a local saloon. Meanwhile, a band of Jackson men loaded all the county archives, seals, and documents into a wagon and whisked the county seat off to Jackson.

But the battles for power and prestige were not over yet. Nearby Mokelumne Hill also wanted to be the county seat, and won the honor through a seemingly up-and-up election, garnering an overwhelming number of votes. It was later determined that the number of ballots cast was several times the number of county residents. This was due to a large band of Mokelumne Hill boosters riding all over the county and voting at every camp and town.

When Mokelumne Hill succeeded in holding the county seat for two terms, the stubborn Jacksonians had had enough, and voted to create a new county—Amador County, one of the state's smallest. Despite the much-improved electoral odds, Jackson barely maintained its status as county seat when challenged by nearby Volcano, but it is still the county seat today.

Jackson's real wealth came not from placer diggings but from hard rock mines such as the Kennedy and Argonaut mines, at one time two of the world's deepest mines. The huge tailing wheels, built to carry waste from the mines to a nearby settling pond, are now the features of the Tailing Wheels Park. There is also a great museum, the Amador County Museum, at 255 Church Street. Look for a red brick house, built in the 1860s and formerly called the Brown House, at the top of a hill about two blocks east of the main part of the town. There is a walking tour of the town, and a map is available at the Amador County Chamber of Commerce at the junction of State Highways 49 and 88.

The Stony Creek, Buena Vista, and Jackson Valley Roads will take you over more rolling Mother Lode terrain and back to Ione.

RIDE GUIDE

    0.0 From Howard Park in Ione, turn right onto SR 124 (Church Street).

    0.3 Turn left onto West Main Street.

    0.4 Turn right onto Preston Avenue.

★   0.5 Turn right onto SR 124 (Plymouth Highway).

★   1.9 Turn right onto Sutter Ione Road.

    8.8 Turn right onto Spanish Street.

★   9.4 Turn right onto SR 49 (Main Street).

★   9.8 Turn left onto Sutter Hill Road.

★ 10.6 Turn right onto Ridge Drive.

★ 10.7 Turn left onto SR 49.

★ 11.6 Turn right onto Argonaut Lane.

★ 12.5 Turn right onto Stony Creek Road.

★ 21.0 Turn right onto Buena Vista Road.

★ 24.0 Turn left onto Jackson Valley Road.

★ 27.6 Ride straight onto Old Stockton Road.

★ 31.6 Turn right onto West Marlette Street.

 33.1 Turn right onto South Buena Vista.

 33.3 Turn right onto Church Street.

 33.7 Howard Park. End of ride.

Region 5

Gold Country

Who needs gold when there are downhills like this? (photo by Gary MacFadden)

Lincoln Loop

29

Submitted by Kurt Sunderbruch

This 21-mile ride starts in the valley before climbing into the scenic Sierra Nevada foothills. There are many great views of the valley farmlands from the lightly traveled two-lane roads.

Type of ride: road bike
Starting point: McBean Park in Lincoln
Finishing point: same
Distance: 21.2 miles round trip
Level of difficulty: moderate
General terrain: mostly level with some rolling hills, two steep climbs
Traffic conditions: light traffic
Estimated riding time: 1.5 to 2.5 hours
Best season/time of day to ride: weekdays
Accommodations and services: all services in Lincoln

GETTING THERE

From Sacramento follow I-80 to Roseville. Take State Highway 65 north 10 miles to Lincoln. Turn right onto State Highway 193 and drive 6 blocks until you see McBean Park on your right. Park in the lot at the northeast corner of the park.

IN THE SADDLE

McBean Park has bathrooms and drinking fountains, so be sure to take advantage of them, as water and services are scarce on the actual loops. To start the ride, cross State Highway 193 and ride onto East Avenue.

This loop ride takes you into the heart of goldmining country in the Doty and Auburn Ravines. Some of the area names (Lincoln, Virginiatown, Auburn) suggest that many of the miners who came to the region were from the midwest and the eastern seaboard. Lonely for their old homes, they often named the new diggings for the towns they left behind.

While Lincoln was an early trading center for a region based on the growing of

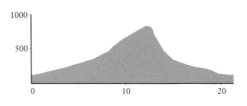

grains and fruits—and later the supply of food and materials for hordes of gold miners—much of the town's economy was based on potterymaking after the 1870s, when the gold was largely played out. The pottery and terracotta works were built at the western edge of the town in huge iron-roofed buildings with imposing smokestacks. One reason for the growth of this industry was the discovery of nearby glass sand and lignite coal deposits by erstwhile gold miners.

As you leave Lincoln on Virginiatown Road, you will pass heaps of dredge tailings left from the mining operations. While much of the gold mined in California was taken in shafts and tunnels like those used in hard-rock mining, two other methods of collecting the gold were common: hydraulic mining and dredging. Both required massive amounts of water, and both methods scarred the landscape for generations.

Hydraulic mining was accomplished by shooting narrow streams of highly pressurized water at a slope where gold deposits were suspected to be present. The heavier metal would wash out and be collected at the bottom of the slope. The dredges were floating barges equipped with large pumps that could suck the mud and rocks

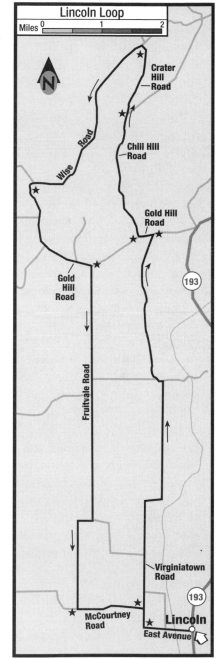

from the bottom of a lake or river; again, the heavier gold would settle out from the lighter materials pulled off of the river and lake bottoms. As the materials were searched and discarded, the dredges left the useless mud and rock behind in large piles, called dredge tailings. In Virginiatown, there is a national historic site containing information about this gold rush town.

After a brief jog onto Gold Hill Road, you will turn right onto Chili Hill Road, which merges onto Crater Hill Road. This is the toughest climb on the route, although cyclists who like to bag high mountain passes will not find it to be overly challenging. This is the Gold Hill Ravine, leading you into the Ophir Mining District. The town of Ophir is just to the southeast of the route as you turn from Crater Hill Road onto Wise Road. Ophir began its community life as Spanish Corral, but changed its name to that of King Solomon's treasure trove when quartz mining began in the late 1840s. By 1852, Ophir was the most populous town in all of Placer County. Today the town is marked only by scars of old shafts, dredge tailings, and stamp mill foundations.

The gold mining towns of this region were born and died quickly. Even in his day, Mark Twain could already write of dozens of ghost towns like Ophir and Gold Hill:

> You will find it hard to believe that here stood at one time a fiercely flourishing little city, of 2,000 or 3,000 souls, with its newspaper, fire company, brass band, volunteer militia, bank, hotels, noisy Fourth of July processions and speeches . . . gambling-halls crammed with tobacco smoke, profanity, and rough-bearded men of all nations and colors, with tables heaped with gold dust . . . labor, laughter, music, swearing, fighting, shooting, stabbing . . . and now nothing but lifeless, homeless solitude. In no other land, in modern times, have towns so absolutely died and disappeared, as in the old mining regions of California.

The difficult climbing is over as you turn onto Wise Road and head back towards Lincoln. At the junction of Gold Hill and Fruitvale Roads (14.3 miles into the ride) is a self-service fruit stand, a good place to get some refreshments.

RIDE GUIDE

0.0 From McBean Park in Lincoln, ride across SR 193 onto East Avenue.

★　0.7 Turn right onto Virginiatown Road.
★　6.6 Turn left onto Gold Hill Road.
★　6.7 Turn right onto Chili Hill Road.
★　8.6 Bear left onto Crater Hill Road.
★　9.8 Turn left onto Wise Road.
★　12.4 Turn left onto Gold Hill Road.
★　14.3 Turn right onto Fruitvale Road.
★　19.4 Turn left onto McCourtney Road.
★　20.4 Turn right onto Virginiatown Road.
★　20.5 Turn left onto East Avenue.
　　21.2 McBean Park. End of Ride.

Downieville Downhill
Submitted by Roger McGehee

Thar's gold in them thar hills—if you place a big value on terrific single-track mountain biking, that is. Actually, the real gold is probably still there, too.

Type of ride: mountain bike
Starting point: Downieville (for shuttle to Butcher Creek trailhead)
Finishing point: Downieville
Distance: 12.7 miles
Level of difficulty: moderate to hard
General terrain: mountainous but downhill
Traffic conditions: other cyclists, few hikers or equestrians, motorcycles on the weekends
Estimated riding time: 2 hours
Best season/time of day to ride: weekdays to avoid motorcycles; late June to September best time since trail usually melts out by mid-June
Points of interest: some great single-track riding
Accommodations and services: food, water, and a bike shop in Downieville
Supplemental maps or other information: Tahoe National Forest map, USDA Forest Service

GETTING THERE

Downieville is located northwest of Lake Tahoe on State Highway 49 (the Gold Rush Highway). Take I-80 north from Sacramento to Grass Valley/Nevada City and pick up State Highway 49 for 32 miles north to Downieville. Park in the downtown area if you are catching a shuttle to the trailhead.

IN THE SADDLE

Downieville is located in the North Yuba River canyon, surrounded by steep hills—everything is up from the town's elevation of 2,700 feet. Major William Downie arrived here in November of 1849 with a party of thirteen. The river was already rimmed with ice, but Downie found the gravels so rich in gold that he immediately began constructing cabins and set about sifting the gravel bars. Supplies ran low, and the party nearly starved to death during the harsh winter. However, they hung on because there was no doubt that the area offered a rich gold deposit.

Secrets are hard to keep, and soon Downieville was a booming metropolis of more than 5,000 miners. On one claim, each of the three miners reportedly filled a tin cup with gold dust every day—this mine became known as the Tin Cup Diggings.

Today the gold has mostly played out, but bikers still have reason to visit because there are several great single-track runs that end in or near Downieville. The Downieville Downhill ride described here is a compilation of two trails: the Butcher Creek Trail and the Third Divide Trail. Check at the bike shop in Downieville for other potential rides. You almost cannot go wrong, but some rides are more technical than others.

Either ride up to the start of the trail (a pretty long, 4,000-foot climb) or have someone shuttle you in a vehicle, which is what most people do. (Shuttle rides are available in Downieville.) If you are using your own vehicle, drive up to Packer Saddle Campground via Gold Lake and Packer Roads (paved). Then ride your bike down the dirt road heading west from the parking area at Packer Saddle Campground. At the Y in the road, turn left and ride up the dirt road. You will see a meadow beginning to form below you on your right. As you approach the top of the ridge, look for a sign that reads, "Butcher Creek OHV Trail." The unsigned trail will turn sharply to the right. This is it: the Butcher Creek Trail.

Intermediate riders should be able to ride most of the Butcher Creek Trail, even though it has some steep and technical sections in it. Do not be afraid to hop off and walk any uncomfortable sections. The trail begins in a red fir forest and passes beside a meadow filled with Mule Ears, through streams lined with columbines, and through several rocky areas. You will come to a junction with the Pauley Creek Trail. (If you have the energy and the time, cross the bridge and pump up a couple of miles and then back down this enjoyable trail.)

OPTION 1 (THIRD DIVIDE TRAIL)
At the junction, move on to the Third Divide Trail. This trail offers some terrific single-track riding and makes it easy to get your speed up above comfortable limits. The surface is very smooth, fast, and fun! Cruise through old-growth forests of ponderosa pine, incense cedar, and Douglas fir. As you approach Downieville, you will reach Lavezzola Road. Take this dirt road into Downieville.

Old general store, downtown Downieville (photo by Gary MacFadden)

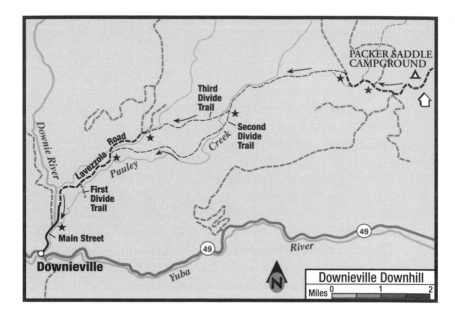

OPTION 2 (SECOND DIVIDE TRAIL)

An alternative ride is to take the Second Divide Trail from the junction with Pauley Creek Trail. The first half of the Second Divide Trail is fast and smooth, but the second half involves lots of technical riding and is very exposed in several places. The Second Divide Trail also comes out onto Lavezzola Road, so take your pick based on your skill level and experience.

Either way, it is downhill to Downieville.

RIDE GUIDE

    0.0 From Packer Saddle Campground parking lot, ride down dirt road.

★ 2.0 At fork, bear to left and ride up unnamed dirt road.

    2.6 As you approach top of ridge, look for "Butcher Creek OHV Trail" sign.

    2.8 Turn right to continue on Butcher Creek Trail.

★ 3.1 Continue straight onto single-track trail (double-track trail goes off to right).

★ 6.1 Trail divides at Pauley Creek.

The Swiss Alps of California (photo by Gary MacFadden)

Option 1 (Third Divide Trail)
★ 6.1 Bear to right.
★ 8.1 Turn left onto Lavezzola Road.
  11.6 Ride onto Main Street.
★ 11.8 Bear left to continue on Main Street.
  12.7 Downieville. End of ride.

Option 2 (Second Divide Trail)
★ 6.1 Bear to left.
★ 9.1 Turn left onto Lavezzola Road.
  11.5 Ride onto Main Street.
★ 11.7 Bear left to continue on Main Street.
  12.6 Downieville. End of ride.

Chico-Durham Loop

Submitted by Ed McLaughlin

This 78-mile road ride of moderate difficulty features lightly traveled rural roads, mining museums, and a Chinese temple, plus lots of wildflower viewing opportunities in the spring.

Type of ride: road bike
Starting point: Chico
Finishing point: same
Distance: 78 miles
Level of difficulty: moderate
General terrain: mostly rolling but good climb to Paradise on Honey Run Road
Traffic conditions: light on two-lane rural roads, heavier on the Dayton-Durham Highway
Estimated riding time: 6 to 8 hours
Best season/time of day to ride: March and April for wildflower viewing
Points of interest: covered bridge on Butte Creek, Chinese temple in Oroville, Cherokee Museum in Cherokee, Gold Nugget Museum in Paradise

Honey Run Covered Bridge, over Butte Creek (photo by Ed McLaughlin)

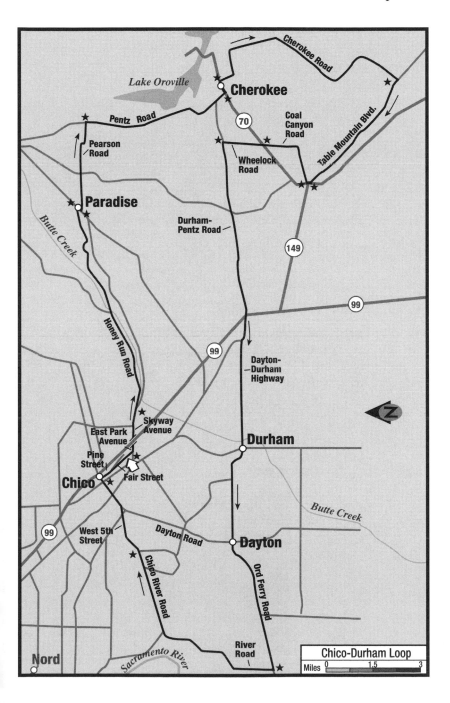

Chico-Durham Loop

Miles 0   1.5   3

Accommodations and services: all services in Chico; food, water, and lodging in Oroville; food and water in Paradise

Supplemental maps or other information: Chico Area Bike Rides map available from Campus Bikes, 501 Main Street, Chico, CA 95928, (916) 345-2081; Chico City map from Chico Visitor and Information Bureau, 500 Main Street, Chico, CA 95928, (800) 852-8570

GETTING THERE

Begin the ride at the Silver Dollar Fairgrounds (parking available) in Chico. Take State Route 99 to Chico and exit at the Skyway (East Park Avenue) exit. Turn west onto East Park to the third signal, which is Fair Street. Turn right and enter the fairgrounds parking lot. Camping and showers are available at the fairgrounds. The ride follows the route used by cyclists each year in April in the Wildflower Century.

IN THE SADDLE

The towns of Chico, Paradise, Cherokee, Oroville, and Durham lie on the edge of the Sierra Nevada foothills. The towns' beginnings are tied to orchards, olives, and gold mining.

In the late 1840s, General John Bidwell, a member of the first overland party to cross the Sierra Nevada, combined the land grants of the Rancho Arroyo Chico and Rancho de Farewell into Rancho Chico. In 1860, when he platted Chico, Bidwell offered free lots to anyone who would homestead on his townsite. Within a decade, Chico was a booming town of 2,000 inhabitants, with churches, hotels, and the ubiquitous gambling houses and saloons.

On his ranch, Bidwell launched experimental orchards that at the time of his death contained more than 400 varieties of fruit. He also pioneered the production of raisins and olives in the region. A 10-acre section of the ranch was donated for the campus of Chico State College; construction began in 1887.

Leave Chico on a gentle run along Butte Creek (do not miss the covered bridge, one of the few remaining bridges of its type). Then begin

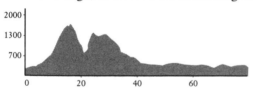

a climb of approximately 1,600 feet in 6 miles on the narrow but generally lightly traveled Honey Run Road toward Paradise.

Chinese temple dedicated in 1863 (photo by Gary MacFadden)

At the top of the climb, cross Skyway Avenue and ride onto Birch Street, then turn right onto Pearson Road.

Pentz Road and a swooping downhill ride will take you south toward Cherokee. After a brief section of State Highway 70, turn onto Cherokee Road and climb over Table Mountain, skirting Lake Oroville. Cherokee is named for a tribe of Cherokee Indians who settled here in 1853 after being forced off their Georgia homelands by gold seekers. The Cherokees found themselves right in the thick of the gold rush once again when the precious metal was discovered in the surrounding foothills. There is a good mining museum in Cherokee.

Thousands of the miners who arrived were Chinese. In 1863, they erected Liet Sheng Kong (Temple of Assorted Deities) at Oroville, just south of the route across the Feather River. The temple was so-named because it was built for worshippers of three different faiths: Confucianism, Buddhism, and Taoism. The temple is both a museum and a place of worship, so please act appropriately when visiting.

Table Mountain Boulevard and Coal Canyon Road (which becomes Wheelock as it crosses State Highway 70) lead you north from Oroville, avoiding the busier State Highway 149. Durham-Pentz Road and Dayton-Durham Highway lead you to Dayton and Old Ferry Road and then right onto River Road back into Chico. (For a shorter ride, you can turn right onto the Durham Bike Path off Dayton-Durham Highway and ride into the Chico city center.)

RIDE GUIDE

    0.0 From Silver Dollar Fairgrounds in Chico, turn left onto Fair Street.

★ 0.2 Turn left onto East Park Avenue.

    0.9 Ride under SR 99. Route becomes Skyway Avenue.

★ 2.3 Turn left onto Honey Run Road.

    6.6 Honey Run Covered Bridge.

★ 12.1 Cross Skyway Avenue and ride onto Birch Street.

★ 12.5 Paradise. Turn left onto Pearson Road.

★ 15.7 Turn right onto Pentz Road.

★ 22.9 Turn left onto SR 70.

★ 23.4 Cherokee. Turn right onto Cherokee Road.

    24.8 Cherokee Mining Era Museum.

★ 35.3 Turn right onto Table Mountain Boulevard.

Pentz Road winding by the Lime Saddle Marina (photo by Ed McLaughlin)

★ 40.9 Turn right onto SR 70.

★ 41.3 Turn right onto Coal Canyon road.

★ 44.5 Cross SR 70 and ride straight onto Wheelock Road.

★ 46.4 Turn left onto Durham-Pentz Road.

53.4 Cross SR 99. Route becomes Dayton-Durham Highway.

58.1 Durham.

58.5 Bear right to continue on Dayton-Durham Highway.

59.4 Bear left to continue on Dayton-Durham Highway.

61.3 Dayton. Cross Dayton Road. Right straight across onto Ord Ferry Road.

★ 66.3 Turn right onto River Road.

71.6 Route becomes Chico River Road.

★ 75.8 Bear left. Route becomes West 5th Street.

★ 77.1 Turn right onto Pine Street.

77.6 At 12th Street, route becomes Mulberry Street; continue straight.

78.0 At 20th Street, route becomes Fair Street; continue straight.

78.5 Silver Dollar Fairgrounds on left. End of ride.

Chimney Rock Trail
Submitted by Curt Ferguson

Here is more great riding in the Downieville area. Unlike the Downieville Downhill (Ride 30), the Chimney Rock Trail is a loop route, so you do not need to arrange for a vehicle shuttle. Hold onto your handlebars, because you have some great downhill single-track ahead!

Type of ride: mountain bike
Starting point: Downieville
Finishing point: same
Distance: 26.4 miles
Level of difficulty: moderate to hard
General terrain: mountainous
Traffic conditions: occasional motorcycles and four-wheel-drive vehicles on OHV portions of the route
Estimated riding time: 4 to 5 hours for a strong rider

Best season/time of day to ride: fall; early in the day in summer; route
closed in spring and winter due to snow conditions
Points of interest: Downieville, an old gold-mining town; Chimney
Rock, a lava extrusion; great views of the Sierras
Accommodations and services: all services in Downieville; camping
nearby
Supplemental maps or other information: Tahoe National Forest
map, USDA Forest Service

GETTING THERE
Downieville is located northwest of Lake Tahoe on State Highway 49
(the Gold Rush Highway). Take I-80 north from Sacramento to Grass
Valley/Nevada City and pick up State Highway 49 for 32 miles north
to Downieville. Park in the downtown area.

IN THE SADDLE
This is a moderate to hard ride. You might want to get a feel for the
area on a shorter ride first; see the Downieville Downhill, Ride 30.

This ride uses several fire roads linked with sections of single-track.
The first section of the ride is climbing, followed by moderate to steep
descents back into Downieville. This is a loop ride beginning and ending in Downieville, so there is no need to arrange for a shuttle.

You will ride the loop in a clockwise direction. The first 10 miles
are on Saddleback Road, a steep fire road, climbing to a scenic fire overlook of the Sierra foothills. At 4.8 miles, the trail levels a bit, with some
rolling hills. At 7 miles, you will pass the Telegraph Mine, a working
gold mine.

At 8.3 miles, there is another scenic overlook. The road here is a
more moderate climb. Bear right and continue climbing. A half-mile
farther up the trail, bear right again (do not continue toward Poker Flat).

At just over 12 miles, enter the Chimney Rock single-track portion
of the ride. This section involves lots of technical riding; watch for rocks
and loose sand. You may be off the bike and pushing at times through
this section. You will pass Chim-
ney Rock, which was formed
from lava eruptions that cooled
into the shape of a chimney.

At the end of the single-track

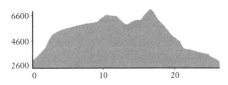

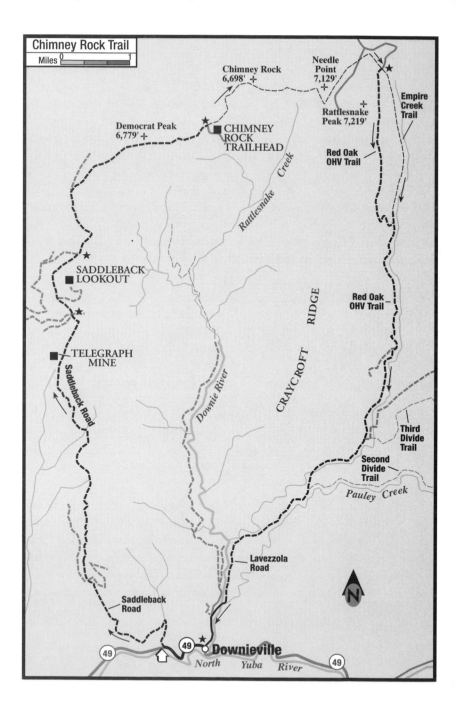

Chimney Rock Trail

Miles 0 — 1

Chimney Rock 6,698'

Needle Point 7,129'

Empire Creek Trail

Rattlesnake Peak 7,219'

Democrat Peak 6,779'

CHIMNEY ROCK TRAILHEAD

Red Oak OHV Trail

Rattlesnake Creek

SADDLEBACK LOOKOUT

Red Oak OHV Trail

TELEGRAPH MINE

Saddleback Road

Downie River

CRAYCROFT RIDGE

Third Divide Trail

Second Divide Trail

Pauley Creek

Lavezzola Road

N

Saddleback Road

49

49

Downieville

North Yuba River

49

portion, you have two choices for the return to Downieville: Empire Creek Trail or Red Oak OHV Trail. Empire Creek Trail is an extreme downhill single-track, while Red Oak OHV Trail is a less extreme fire road. Take your pick, because the trails parallel each other until Empire Creek eventually hooks up with Red Oak, which leads back to Lavezzola Road and Downieville.

The peak elevation on the climb is 6,760 feet, just before Chimney Rock trail threads between Rattlesnake Peak (elevation 7,219 feet) and Needle Peak (elevation 7,129 feet).

Carry adequate water supplies for the 4 to 5 hours you will be on the road, because no water is available en route. If doing this ride during the summer months, get an early start to avoid the heat.

RIDE GUIDE

    0.0 From trailhead on SR 49, ride north on Saddleback Road.

    7.0 Telegraph Mine.

★   8.3 Bear right to continue on route.

★   8.7 Bear right to continue on route.

★ 12.3 Ride onto Chimney Rock Trail.

  13.3 Chimney Rock.

★ 15.9 End of single-track portion. Either ride onto Empire Creek Trail or bear right onto Red Oak OHV Trail.

★ 25.8 Downieville. Turn right onto SR 49.

  26.4 Trailhead. End of ride.

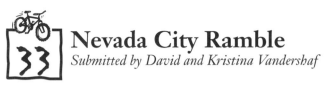

33 Nevada City Ramble
Submitted by David and Kristina Vandershaf

This 45-mile mountain biking route offers a variety of rides in the Sierra foothills, from fire road climbs to single-track descents.

Type of ride: mountain bike or sturdy road bike
Starting point: Nevada City
Finishing point: same
Distance: 45 miles
Level of difficulty: moderate

General terrain: rolling, with two steep climbs out of river drainages
Traffic conditions: mostly light on rural roads
Estimated riding time: 5 to 6 hours
Best season/time of day to ride: spring through fall
Points of interest: walking/cycling tours in Nevada City and Grass
    Valley; North Star Mining Museum; covered bridge at Bridgeport
Accommodations and services: all services in Grass Valley and Nevada
    City; food and water in smaller towns along route
Supplemental maps or other information: Nevada City Chamber of
    Commerce, 132 Main Street, Nevada City, CA 95959, (916) 265-2692

GETTING THERE

Take I-80 north from Sacramento to Grass Valley/Nevada City. Take
State Highway 49 and exit at Broad Street. There is a public parking
area, complete with bathrooms and drinking water, on the east side of
State Highway 49.

IN THE SADDLE

This road mixes paved (mostly) and dirt roads for a fun loop ride in the
historic Nevada City area. You could do this tour on a sturdy touring
bike, but because of the dirt and gravel roads, a mountain bike is probably the best choice.

From the public parking area, go through the freeway interchange
(pay attention to traffic—it is busy here) and climb Broad Street, straight
into the downtown district of Nevada City.

Broad Street reaches a fork; go right onto East Broad Street. At mile
0.8, cross State Highway 49 at a two-way stop and continue straight
ahead on North Bloomfield Road. At mile 1.4, turn right at a т intersection. At mile 5.8, you will be at the highest elevation of the tour: 3,060
feet. The traffic thins and the road narrows. Begin dropping steeply
toward the South Yuba River.

At mile 8.5, reach the Edwards Crossing Bridge at the South Yuba
River. This is a popular recreation
area for hiking and river activities.
The road turns to dirt and climbs
steeply up the other side of the canyon, away from the river. At mile 10,
turn onto Grizzly Hill Road, still

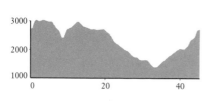

riding on dirt. In another 3 miles, return to pavement, still on Grizzly Hill Road. Shortly thereafter, turn left onto Tyler-Foote Road.

At mile 18.2, reach the junction with Oak Tree Road. Here you will find the first grocery store since leaving Nevada City. At the junction, turn right onto Oak Tree Road. Two miles later, reach the small town of North San Juan. This town has two stores and a restaurant, which makes it a good lunch stop.

At the west end of North San Juan (you arrived on the east end), turn right onto Sweetland Road, which is partially dirt. At mile 23.7, turn right onto Pleasant Valley Road. You will get a delightful down-hill to another crossing at the South Yuba River and the lowest eleva-tion of the trip at 570 feet. The shingle-sided covered bridge at Bridgeport is, at 233 feet long, one of the longest single-span covered

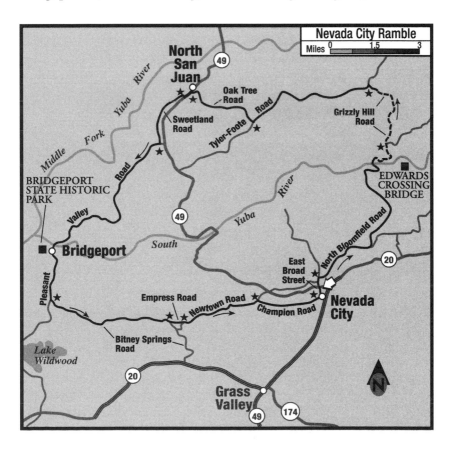

bridges in the United States and is a state historic monument.

Note that Bridgeport, which has an adequate parking area for recreational traffic, would make a good alternate starting point for this ride, enabling you to complete your biggest climb early in the ride.

As you leave Bridgeport, begin climbing back toward Nevada City.

This wheel powered the North Star Mine. (photo by Gary MacFadden)

There are several turns in a short amount of mileage, so check the Ride Guide carefully. At mile 33.2, turn left onto Bitney Springs Road; at mile 38.3, turn left onto Empress Road. At mile 38.9, turn left onto Newtown Road, and at mile 41.7, turn right onto Champion Road. This last road is mostly dirt, but it avoids heavy traffic and a steep hill.

At mile 44.3, turn right onto Old Downieville Road; a half-mile later, now in Nevada City, you will turn right onto Spring Street, left onto South Pine Street, and right onto Broad Street and back to the parking area.

If you have some time to spend in the Nevada City/Grass Valley area, take advantage of the walking tours in the two communities; brochures are available at the Chamber of Commerce in Nevada City. You might also enjoy the mining equipment display and historical artifacts at the North Star Mining Museum in Grass Valley, located at the end of Mill Street, near the junction of McCourtney and Allison Ranch Roads.

RIDE GUIDE

0.0 From public parking area on SR 49 in Nevada City, ride north on Broad Street.

0.4 Bear right onto East Broad Street.

★ 0.8 Cross SR 49 and ride onto North Bloomfield Road.

★ 1.4 At the T, turn right to continue on North Bloomfield Road.

8.5 South Yuba River and Edwards Crossing Bridge.

★ 10.0 Turn left onto Grizzly Hill Road.

★ 13.2 Turn left onto Tyler-Foote Road.

★ 18.2 Turn right onto Oak Tree Road.

21.0 North San Juan. Turn left onto SR 49.

★ 21.2 Turn right onto Sweetland Road.

★ 23.7 Turn right onto Pleasant Valley Road.

30.6 South Yuba River. Bridgeport.

★ 33.2 Turn left onto Bitney Springs Road.

★ 38.3 Turn left onto Empress Road.

★ 38.9 Turn left onto Newtown Road.

★ 41.7 Turn right onto Champion Road.

44.3 Turn right onto Old Downieville Road.

44.9 Turn right onto Spring Street, then immediately left onto South Pine Street, then right onto Broad Street.

45.1 Parking lot. End of ride.

Gold Lake Ride
Submitted by James Hardy

High mountain lakes that once attracted thousands of gold seekers, jagged peaks reminiscent of the Austrian Alps, and some serious climbing (and the downhills that follow) are all part of this ride.

Type of ride: road bike
Starting point: Graeagle
Ending point: same
Distance: 50 miles
Level of difficulty: moderate
General terrain: several significant climbs but otherwise rolling
Traffic conditions: very light along all portions of the ride
Estimated riding time: 6 to 8 hours
Best season/time of day to ride: mid-May to mid-September; less traffic during the week
Points of interest: Gold Lake, the Sierra Buttes, old stage station
Accommodations and services: camping, groceries, restaurants, motel/ B&B, parking along the route

GETTING THERE
Begin the ride in Graeagle, on the middle fork of the Feather River. Graeagle, surrounded on three sides by the Plumas National Forest, is just off State Highway 70 as you drive toward Reno. From Sacramento, travel east on I-80 for approximately 110 miles, then turn north on State Highway 89; Graeagle is located 40 miles away.

IN THE SADDLE
Ride east out of Graeagle on State Highway 89 for 2 miles, then turn right onto Golden Lake Forest Highway. For the next 10 miles, climb to Gold Lake Summit, passing Gold Lake just before reaching the crest.

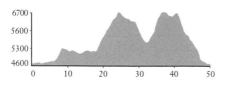

Gold Lake gained fame during the gold rush days for the nuggets rumored to be lying on its alpine shores, just waiting for some lucky miner to stoop down

Climbing to the summit from Bassets (photo by James Hardy)

This popular bed and breakfast was originally a stagecoach hotel built in 1850. (photo by Gary MacFadden)

and scoop them up. It makes a good place to stop during the climb, and—who knows?—you might get lucky.

At Gold Lake Summit, you will be looking southeast to the Sierra Buttes, a jagged skyline reminiscent of the Austrian Alps, usually covered with snow. These mountains are rich in California gold rush history, and there are still several active gold mines in the area. Around 9.8 miles, the route becomes Gold Lake Road.

There is a 6.5-mile downhill waiting to take you to Bassetts, a small resort community with a motel, country store, and cafe, situated at the junction of Golden Lake Forest Highway and State Highway 49 (also known as the Mother Lode Road). Yuba Pass is still ahead, so you might as well take a break.

Leaving Bassetts, turn northeast on State Highway 49 and climb the 8-mile Yuba Grade. Your route parallels the crystal-clear, freezing-cold Yuba River to an elevation of just over 6,700 feet. From Yuba Pass, you can see into the Sierra Valley and northeast into Nevada.

Now you face another steep downhill, this one with plenty of switchbacks where you might run over yourself if not careful. Test your brakes and keep your speed under control. There are a couple of great vista overlooks along the way, which provide another reason to keep your speed down.

At the bottom of the grade, turn left onto State Highway 89. In about a mile, you will pass an old sawmill, complete with the remains of a teepee burner. These were used to burn sawdust and lumber waste before anyone thought of making paper and cardboard out of the by-products of the lumber industry.

In another 3 miles, you will pass through the little settlement of Calpine. Remain on State Highway 89 and make a final climb of 500 feet over the Calpine Summit. As you continue toward Graeagle, you

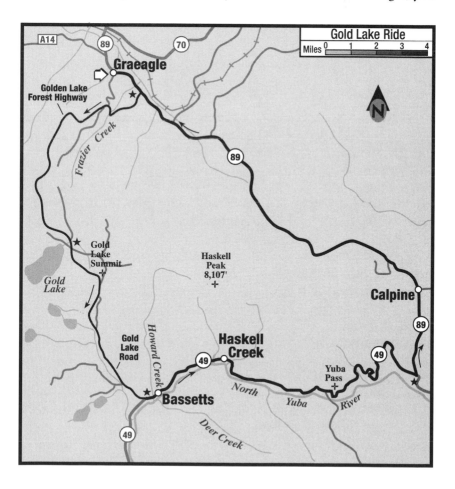

will pass a stagecoach hotel built in 1850 that is now a beautiful bed and breakfast. Some of the furnishings are original, and the friendly owners have added other antiques. (This is a good place to begin and end this ride.)

From here it is an easy 5 miles through rolling woodlands and beautiful green valleys to Graeagle and the end of the ride.

RIDE GUIDE

    0.0 From Graeagle, ride east on SR 89.

★   2.0 Turn right onto Golden Lake Forest Highway.

★   9.8 Route becomes Gold Lake Road.

★ 18.6 Bassetts. Turn left onto SR 49.

★ 33.3 Turn left onto SR 89.

  36.3 Calpine.

  50.2 Graeagle. End of ride.

Sutter Buttes
Submitted by Richard Peters

Ride around the "world's smallest mountain range" in just a long morning on this easy loop route where you can use either your road or mountain bike.

Type of ride: road bike
Starting point: Sutter
Finishing point: same
Distance: 40.2 miles
Level of difficulty: easy
General terrain: flat
Traffic conditions: light along rural roads
Estimated riding time: 3 to 5 hours
Best season/time of day to ride: April, May
Points of interest: "world's smallest mountain range"; rock walls built by Chinese laborers
Accommodations and services: few services along the route away from Sutter

The Buttes as seen from the west (photo by Richard Peters)

GETTING THERE
From Yuba City, 45 miles north of Sacramento on State Highway 70/99, go 4 miles west on State Highway 20, then right on Acacia Avenue 2 miles to Sutter. The ride begins at the parking lot of the Sutter Union High School on the west side of Acacia Avenue.

IN THE SADDLE
This is an easy, generally flat road bike ride that circumnavigates what is locally referred to as the "world's smallest mountain range," the Sutter Buttes. The Buttes—the only peaks on California's vast interior plain—are a unique volcanic formation that rises in the middle of the Sacramento Valley. Of the four jagged peaks, South Butte (elevation 2,128 feet) is the highest. The buttes are the eroded remains of a crater that formerly rose to twice the present height.

It is fun (and maybe impressive) to tell friends that you biked around a volcanic mountain range in a single morning. The 40-mile loop can be done in as little as 3 hours, but allow additional time for a more leisurely ride.

There are no food or water services along the route, so take along extra water bottles and some snacks.

The traffic is light, but the road has several sections where the pavement is badly broken. These sections last for only a few hundred yards; most of the bad areas are on the west and northwest sides of the Buttes.

189

On the west side, the road generally follows the edges of the Buttes where they touch the valley floor. On the other three sides, the road boxes the range from a distance. You will ride through orchards and rice paddies on all four sides.

This ride is best done in the spring, around the first part of April, when the wildflowers are abundant and the weather sunny but still reasonably cool.

Interesting features to watch for are the many low walls, built of stacked volcanic rock. In the years following the gold rush, local farmers employed Chinese laborers to build these walls that are in ways reminiscent of those found in New England. (Records show that the laborers were paid 5 cents per day.)

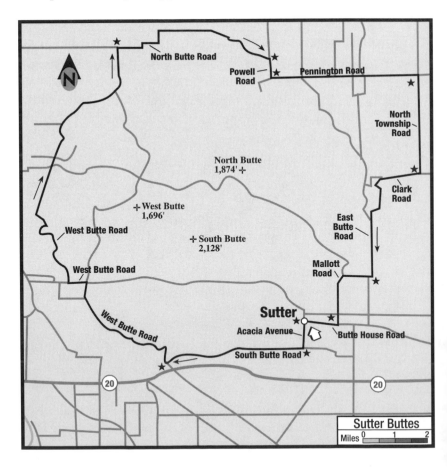

Sutter Buttes, the "world's smallest mountain range" (photo by Gary MacFadden)

The Buttes themselves are on private property, which is why this is a road bike ride. There are bike route marker signs at many of the intersections, and the turns are well-signed. If you miss a sign, remember that you want to remain on South, West, North, and East Butte Roads for most of the ride. The final segment is on Butte House Road back to Acacia Avenue and Sutter.

RIDE GUIDE

    0.0 From Sutter Union High School parking lot, ride south on Acacia Avenue.

★ 0.6 Turn right onto South Butte Road.

★ 4.9 Turn right onto West Butte Road.

    9.1 Turn left to remain on West Butte Road.

    9.7 Turn right to remain on West Butte Road.

★ 18.7 Turn right onto North Butte Road.

★ 24.2 Turn right onto Powell Road.

★ 24.7 Turn left onto Pennington Road.

★ 29.3 Turn right onto North Township road.

★ 32.0 Turn right onto Clark Road.

  35.2 Route becomes East Butte Road.

★ 36.8 Turn right onto Mallott Road.

★ 39.1 Turn right onto Butte House Road.

★ 40.1 Turn left onto Acacia Avenue.

  40.2 Sutter Union High School parking lot. End of ride.

Mount Lola Peak

Submitted by Jim Haagen-Smit

This moderate-to-hard mountain bike ride will take you to the top of Mount Lola Peak in the High Sierra, with a 360-degree view of other peaks and high-mountain lakes.

Type of ride: mountain bike
Starting point: Little Truckee Summit OHV Trailhead
Finishing point: same (alternates noted in text)
Distance: 23 miles (or less with alternates)

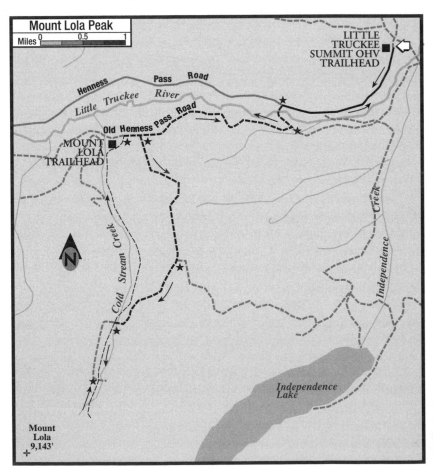

Level of difficulty: lower portions of ride fine for novices; upper stretches for intermediate to advanced

General terrain: flat to rolling on lower stretches; mountainous on upper sections

Traffic conditions: light to nonexistent

Estimated riding time: 4 to 6 hours (can be done in fewer than 3 hours by a strong rider not interested in scenery)

Best season/time of day to ride: August until the first snowfall (usually October); can be ridden as early as July in drought years

Points of interest: unparalleled views of High Sierra Nevada peaks and lakes

Accommodations and services: campgrounds in Tahoe National Forest; B&B and motels in nearby historic rail town of Truckee

Supplemental maps or other information: USGS quad for Donner Pass; USDA Forest Service Tahoe National Forest map, Mount Diablo Meridian

GETTING THERE

This ride begins at the Little Truckee Summit OHV Trailhead, with a large parking area, toilets, and picnic spot. The trailhead is 15.8 miles north of the Truckee/I-80 exit from State Highway 89. Turn left (west) off State Highway 89 at the Independence Lake/Webber Lake sign.

IN THE SADDLE

Ride out of the parking lot and onto the paved Henness Pass Road for 1.3 miles, then turn left onto a dirt road signed "Independence Lake—5 miles." At 1.5 miles, a metal-decked bridge takes you over the Little Truckee River.

At 2.0 miles, turn right at a four-way intersection onto the Old Henness Pass Road. This was an old stage route across the Sierra Crest. (If you continue straight, you will come to the beautiful Independence Lake, which is ringed by private property. Ask permission if anyone is at the small store there if you can sit lakeside for a few moments to soak in the scenery. The view will only cost you a 4-mile round trip from the turn onto Old Henness Pass Road. Beginning riders can use this alternate as an easy 11-mile out-and-back ride from the Little Truckee Summit parking lot.)

The next couple of miles on the Old Henness Pass Road are along an open dirt road, with aspens edging private rangelands interspersed with sections of the Tahoe National Forest. At 5.1 miles, you will see a dirt road to the left (south). This is the recommended route to the summit of Mount Lola. However, the official trailhead is still ahead on Old Henness Pass Road, in a small parking lot on the left at about 5.3 miles. There should be a sign, but at last check, the post was standing without the sign. (To shorten this ride, you can drive to this trailhead and park.)

If you choose to climb Mount Lola from the official trailhead, keep in mind that the initial section is fairly technical single-track riding. However, it is still a climb, no matter which choice you make. Get in a low gear and pace yourself for a 2.1-mile climb.

Bear right at the T at the top of the ridge (at 7.8 miles). Then cruise along with more down than up for just over a mile until you cross a wooden bridge over Cold Stream Creek. A few hundred feet after the bridge, carefully search for trail markings—a small silver diamond and blaze—on a large tree on the left side of the dirt road. This marks the single-track leading left (south) to Mount Lola. You should find this turn onto single-track at about the 9-mile point in the ride.

For the next 2 miles, this lovely trail winds through the trees and a meadow as it follows the meandering Cold Stream Creek. Cross the road that you were on earlier at about the 10-mile point; the trail picks up on the other side of the road just a little to the right.

The trail steepens now. You have climbed to an elevation of 8,000 feet (2,000 feet since the Little Truckee Summit OHV Trailhead parking lot). You will encounter a couple of small stream crossings in this section of the ride. At 10.8 miles, as the trail turns to the left, you should hear a nice 20-foot waterfall up and to your right. Hike over for a closer look and a breather from the climbing.

Even in August, you may encounter snow in shaded portions of the trail at this point. At approximately 11 miles, turn up a wide switchback that swings to the right (east) toward Mount Lola. If you are not insistent about taking your bike all the way to the summit, stash it in the trees and hike the rest of the way with just your lunch and camera. It is a fine 15-minute hike (or bike push) from the switchback, with outstanding vistas.

At the summit, you will see Castle Peak to the south, Old Man Mountain to the west, Sierra Valley to the north, and Independence

You may encounter snow year-round. (photo by Jim Haagen-Smit)

Lake and Stampede Reservoirs to the east. White Rock Lake sits just below the summit to the west.

Now you have a quite rideable descent that will have you grinning from ear to ear. Depending upon whether you stashed your bike or took it up to the peak, your mileage will be between 13.5 and 14.0 miles when you reach the bridge at Cold Stream Creek. Cross the bridge and climb the road 50 feet or so, searching for a trail marking and small arrow on the trees that indicate the start of the trail down to the official Mount Lola Trailhead. Descend this trail along the east side of Cold Stream Creek for approximately 2 miles. Most of this trail is rideable, but there are a few steep, rocky sections that you might want to walk.

At about the 16-mile point, you will pop out into the small trailhead parking lot. Then simply retrace the 5.3 miles back on the dirt road to the Old Henness Pass Road and the Little Truckee Summit OHV Trailhead parking lot. You might decide to stay overnight—campgrounds are available in the vicinity. Stay only in designated campgrounds, since it is difficult to tell if land along the roads is part of the national forest or is private.

RIDE GUIDE

    0.0 From Little Truckee Summit OHV Trailhead, ride right onto Henness Pass Road.

★   1.3 Turn left onto unnamed dirt road, signed "Independence Lake—5 miles."

    1.5 Little Truckee River.

★   2.0 Turn right onto Old Henness Pass Road.

★   5.1 Turn left onto unnamed dirt road.

★   7.8 At T, turn right at top of ridge.

    8.8 Cross Cold Stream Creek.

★   9.0 Turn left onto single-track trail. Watch for trail marking (small silver diamond and blaze) on a large tree on left side of road.

    10.0 Cross dirt road.

    10.8 Turn left to continue on trail.

    11.0 Turn right up a wide switchback.

    11.4 Mount Lola Summit. Turnaround point.

★   13.6 Cold Stream Creek. After crossing bridge, ride approximately 50 feet and look for trail marking. Turn and ride down to Mount Lola Trailhead.

    16.0 Turn right from trailhead parking lot.

★   19.3 Turn right onto Old Henness Pass Road.

    19.8 Little Truckee River.

★   20.0 Turn left onto unnamed dirt road.

★   20.7 Turn right onto Henness Pass Road.

    23.0 Little Truckee Summit OHV parking lot. End of ride.

Bullards Bar Loop
Submitted by Jim Haagen-Smit

This 68-mile loop in the foothills of the Sierra Nevada gold country features visits to the huge dam at Bullards Bar Reservoir and the Bridgeport covered bridge on many lightly traveled roads.

Type of ride: road bike with wider tires; not racing wheels due to several sections of dirt and gravel

Starting point: Park 'n' Ride lot 7 miles west of Grass Valley

Finishing point: same

Distance: 67.6 miles

Level of difficulty: moderate

General terrain: rolling hills, drops to several river crossings

Traffic conditions: light on rural roads; several stretches on busier highways

Estimated riding time: 5 to 7 hours

Best season/time of day to ride: October through May; hot summer weekends bring out boat trailers on several sections

Points of interest: small gold-mining towns; Bridgeport State Historic Park; dam at Bullards Bar Reservoir

Accommodations and services: small stores and camping along route; bike service in nearby Nevada City

Supplemental maps or other information: Compass map for Nevada/ Sierra Counties, available at several of the stores en route

GETTING THERE

Begin this ride at a Park 'n' Ride lot just west of Grass Valley, a small hard rock mining town in the Sierra Nevada foothills. Take I-80 north from Sacramento to Grass Valley/Nevada City. Turn west onto State Highway 20 and drive approximately 7 miles to the intersection with Pleasant Valley Road. The parking lot is on the south side of State Highway 20.

IN THE SADDLE

Ride or walk across State Highway 20 from the parking lot. There is a small shopping center where you can pick up supplies for the ride (one of your best food selections on the route, as well as the most reliable—you cannot depend on other stores being open). Ride north on Pleasant Valley Road, through rolling terrain, passing over the dam for the Lake Wildwood Reservoir. A gradual climb will take you past homes scattered along the edge of the lake.

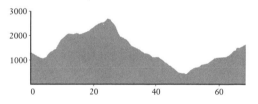

The pavement ends, and you will have a bumpy descent to the Bridgeport State Historic Park. Crossing the South Yuba River is a shingle-sided covered bridge; at 233 feet long, it is one of the longest single-span covered bridges in the United States. The park features a short nature walk and a small visitor center. There are also toilets available.

Steel yourself for the climb out of the Yuba River canyon, still on Pleasant Valley Road. Pass through what is left of French Corral—the oldest town on San Juan Ridge—and Birchville. The first long-distance telephone line in the West was strung between Milton and French Corral to connect the two mining centers.

Continue on Pleasant Valley Road to the junction with State Highway 49; turn left on State Highway 49 and ride approximately 2 miles into North San Juan. There are several small stores here, and it is a good place to grab a snack.

No one is sure how North San Juan got its name. The most likely explanation is that when Mexican War veteran Christian Kientz discovered gold on the nearby ridge in 1853, he saw a resemblance between this area and the battlefield of San Juan de Ulloa in Mexico. Whatever the reason, the San Juan Ridge workings attracted some 10,000 miners and support crews in very short order. In later years, the community attracted several of the Beat Poets such as Gary Snyder and Allen Ginsberg, as well as a couple of long-running communes.

You will have a fast descent on Highway 49 for approximately 2 miles to the crossing of the Middle Fork of the Yuba River. Slow down because your left-hand turn onto Moonshine Road happens immediately after you cross the bridge! Moonshine Road is bumpy, but the quiet, shaded road is a welcome change of pace from the busier State Highway 49. Climb a little as you follow Moonshine Road about 3 miles to the T intersection with Marysville Road.

Turn left (west) onto Marysville Road and follow the smooth pavement for another downhill run to the North Fork of the Yuba River and the Bullards Bar Reservoir dam. This dam is huge; the spillway drops over 500 feet to the river below. After heavy rains, the water releases from the dam can be spectacular.

You can continue your ride west on Marysville Road or take a scenic detour (with some stiff climbing) up Road 169. To find it, after crossing the dam, turn right and up the hill into a parking lot. Ride to the end of the lot; you will see a small and very steep road. Climb away! The road flattens a little as you pass several old outbuildings. Continue climbing the tree-shaded slopes to an intersection with the wider Oregon House Road. Turn left onto Oregon House and follow it to the intersection where you rejoin Marysville Road, the end of the optional detour.

You will have a smooth descent into the town of Dobbins. Again, keep the speed down at the bottom of the grade, because you have a turn to the left onto Texas Hill Road after the runaway truck ramp. Dobbins may have a store open; this is the last food stop available on the loop, and it is not very dependable.

Texas Hill Road rejoins Marysville Road in about 5 miles. At the

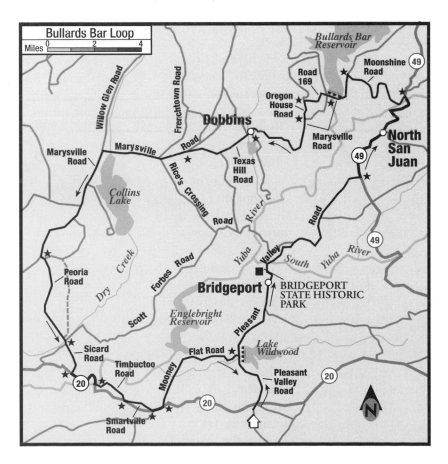

junction, turn left onto Marysville Road. In approximately 7 miles, you
will come to a T with a stop sign. Marysville Road turns to the left (south)
towards Marysville. Stay on Marysville Road for another 7 miles; the
traffic will increase through this section.

Watch for a left-hand turn onto Peoria Road—it is an easy turn to
miss. If you reach Fruitlan Road on your right, you have gone too far.
Peoria Road is narrow and bumpy, but it leaves the car traffic behind.
Proceed south on Peoria for 5 miles; about 0.75 mile after crossing a
bridge over a small creek, turn left onto Sicard Road. This will take you
to State Highway 20, a busy two-lane highway with wide shoulders. Turn
left onto State Highway 20 and head back toward Grass Valley. Cross
the new bridge over the Yuba River.

Here you have a choice of taking a quicker route back to the parking
lot by staying on State Highway 20 (with more traffic) or of combining
a couple of rural roads (with some dirt stretches) for a quieter, more
scenic, and slightly longer ride. If you decide on the scenic route, turn
right at the end of the new bridge and descend under the bridge onto
an old, old road. Head east toward the small towns of Timbuctoo and
Smartville (yes, there really is a Timbuctoo). Right after Timbuctoo,
ride on State Highway 20, turning left again in a few hundred yards back
onto the old road to Smartville.

After Smartville, turn left again onto State Highway 20 for less than
a mile before turning left at the signpost for Englebright Reservoir and
Mooney Flat Road. Mooney Flat is smooth and wide until you pass the
entrance to the Reservoir. After that, it turns to dirt, but most road bikers
enjoy this smooth stretch that climbs gradually away from the dam at
Lake Wildwood. Turn right at the dam onto Pleasant Valley Road, the
road on which you started this loop. Pleasant Valley will take you back
up to State Highway 20 and the parking lot.

RIDE GUIDE

    0.0 From Park 'n' Ride parking lot on SR 20, ride north on
        Pleasant Valley Road.

    5.6 Bridgeport. Bridgeport State Historic Park.

★ 11.3 Turn left onto SR 49.

★ 15.8 North San Juan. Turn left onto Moonshine Road.

★ 20.3 Turn left onto Marysville Road.

   21.1 Bullards Bar Reservoir dam.

★ 21.5 Turn right and ride through parking lot onto Road 169.
★ 22.4 Turn left onto Oregon House Road.
★ 23.3 Ride straight onto Marysville Road.
★ 27.4 Dobbins. Turn left onto Texas Hill Road.
★ 31.3 Turn left onto Marysville Road.
    35.2 Turn left to continue on Marysville Road.
★ 41.2 Turn left onto Peoria Road.
★ 47.3 Turn left onto Sicard Road.
★ 49.3 Turn left onto SR 20.
★ 51.3 Turn left onto Timbuctoo Road.
★ 53.1 Turn left onto SR 20.
    53.3 Turn left onto Smartville Road.
★ 59.1 Turn left onto SR 20.
★ 59.3 Turn left onto Mooney Flat Road.
★ 65.0 Turn right onto Pleasant Valley Road.
    67.6 Park 'n' Ride parking lot. End of ride.

Dutch Flat

38

Submitted by Earle Reynolds

This low-traffic, scenic route will take you from historic Auburn through colorful Colfax and up to Dutch Flat with an optional out-and-back tour through a beautiful canyon.

Type of ride: road ride
Starting point: Park 'n' Ride lot near Auburn
Finishing point: same
Distance: 73 miles round trip (62 miles without optional ride to dam)
Level of difficulty: moderate, with a total of 4,900 feet of climbing
General terrain: mountainous
Traffic conditions: light except on short portions of State Highway 174
Estimated riding time: 5 hours
Best season/time of day to ride: May through October; avoid Colfax and Dutch Flat celebrations on Memorial Day and July 4th
Points of interest: small gold-mining towns with museums; Power Drum Canyon and dam

A gold mining museum in Dutch Flat (photo by Earle Reynolds)

Accommodations and services: food and water in most towns
Supplemental maps or other information: Compass map for Western Placer County

GETTING THERE

On I-80 northeast of Sacramento, take the Bowman Exit into Auburn. From the center of Auburn (not large) go east approximately 3 miles to Bowman Road, to a well-marked Park 'n' Ride lot.

IN THE SADDLE

While in Auburn, check out Old Town and the large monuments honoring the early gold miners and railroad laborers. History buffs will want to allow extra time.

From the Park 'n' Ride lot east of Auburn, cross under the I-80 overpass and right onto Bowman Road. Turn right onto Dry Creek Road at the 2-mile point. At the 3.5-mile point, stay straight as the road becomes Lake Arthur Road and then Crother Road. At the intersection, turn right onto Placer Hills Road.

If you are looking for restroom facilities at the 10-mile point, drop down to the Bear River Campground—you will have to climb back out to Placer Hills Road. Continue on Placer Hills Road approximately 5 miles past the campground turnoff, onto Tokayana Way and into Shady Glen. You have already climbed 2,000 feet at this point, so Shady Glen makes a good place to take a break.

In Shady Glen, turn right onto Old Tokayana Way, right onto Church Street, and left onto Main Street. Leave Shady Glen on State Highway 174 (with higher traffic) and watch for your right turn onto Rollins Lake Road at the edge of town.

Your next challenge is Norton Grade Road, the toughest stretch of the ride. Fortunately, it is well-shaded and you will at least stay cool as you climb the grade that is never more than 6 to 7 percent. As you climb the grade, on your left are the effects of placer mining over the years. The hydraulic sprays tore away at the hillsides and permanently scarred the landscape.

After Magra Road and the small town of Gold Run, at the 28-mile point, you will find that you have earned a terrific downhill into Dutch Flat. Keep some climbing reserves, because at the bottom of the hill you have a climb with an 8 percent grade into the town of Dutch Flat.

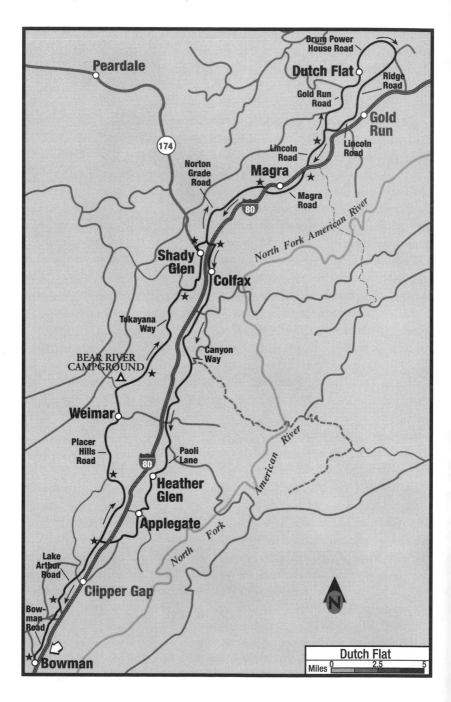

Peardale

Drum Power
House Road

Dutch Flat

Ridge
Road

Gold Run
Road

Gold
Run

174

Lincoln
Road

Lincoln
Road

Norton
Grade
Road

Magra

Magra
Road

North Fork American River

80

Shady
Glen

Colfax

Tokayana
Way

Canyon
Way

BEAR RIVER
CAMPGROUND

Weimar

American River

Placer
Hills
Road

Paoli
Lane

80

Heather
Glen

Applegate

North Fork

Lake
Arthur
Road

Clipper Gap

Bow-
map
Road

N

Bowman

Dutch Flat

Miles   0   2.5   5

This is a fun gold-mining town to visit because, unlike the majority of mining camps, Dutch Flat was never ravaged by fire. Many of its business buildings and homes are original. You might want to check out the Golden Drift Museum, right across from the post office.

You can return to Colfax and Auburn from this point or take an optional out-and-back ride along the Drum Power House Road into a beautiful canyon. This road is owned by Pacific Gas and Electric. The ride down to the dam is 7 miles one way, but you will lose only 500 feet in elevation. Ask permission at the powerhouse to use the picnic table next to the river. When you are rested, head back out to Alta and Dutch Flat.

You might choose to ride around Alta, the highest point of this ride. Most of your ride back to Auburn will be downhill, except for the short climb up to Norton Grade Road. Enjoy!

RIDE GUIDE
0.0 From Bowman Park 'n' Ride lot, ride under I-80.
★ 0.1 Turn right onto Bowman Road.
2.1 Turn right onto Dry Creek Road.

Not all of the Dutch Flat loop is flat. (photo by Earle Reynolds)

★   3.5 Ride straight onto Lake Arthur Road which becomes
    Crother Road.
★   7.5 Turn right onto Placer Hills Road.
★ 12.8 Ride straight onto Tokayana Way.
★ 14.9 Turn right onto Old Tokayana Way.
    15.1 Turn right onto Church Street.
    15.3 Turn left onto Main Street.
    15.4 Shady Glen.
    15.7 Turn left onto SR 174.

One of the local attractions along the route (photo by Earle Reynolds)

★ 16.6 Turn right onto Rollins Lake Road.

17.9 Turn right onto Glen Alder Road.

18.0 Turn left onto Norton Grade Road.

★ 20.8 Turn left at stop sign and then immediately right onto Magra Road.

24.8 Turn right onto Gold Run Road.

25.2 Turn left onto Lincoln Road.

27.0 Turn left onto Ridge Street.

27.2 Turn left onto Sacramento Street.

28.2 Turn right onto Main Street.

29.0 Dutch Flat.

29.6 Turn left onto unnamed street and then left onto Drum Power House Road.

43.1 Turn left onto Mary Red Road.

43.5 Turn right onto Alta Bonnynook Road.

43.9 Turn right onto Ridge Road.

43.9 Gold Run

45.8 Turn right onto Lincoln Road.

47.5 Turn right onto Gold Run Road.

★ 48.0 Turn left onto Magra Road.

52.1 Ride straight onto Rollins Lake Road.

54.9 Turn left onto Glen Alder Road.

★ 55.0 Turn right onto Norton Grade Road.

56.1 Turn left onto Rollins Lake Road.

56.4 Turn left onto SR 174.

57.9 Turn left onto Auburn Road.

58.0 Turn left and cross I-80.

★ 58.1 Turn right onto Canyon Way.

63.1 Turn right onto Paoli Lane.

63.3 Turn right onto West Paoli Lane.

63.5 Turn right onto Geisendorfer Road.

64.9 Turn left onto Applegate Road.

★ 69.3 Turn left onto Lake Arthur Road.

69.4 Turn left onto Applegate Road.

69.3 Turn right onto Placer Hills Road.

69.4 Turn left onto Lake Arthur Road.

★ 70.9 Turn left onto Bowman Road.

72.8 Bowman. End of ride.

39 Lake Davis Loop
Submitted by Allen Kost

This is an easy family ride around pristine Lake Davis, located just north of Portola. It features some great vistas as well as bird and wildlife viewing.

Type of ride: road bike
Starting point: Lake Davis Dam
Finishing point: same
Distance: 18.4 miles
Level of difficulty: easy
General terrain: level
Traffic conditions: light traffic, heavier on the weekends
Estimated riding time: 2 hours
Best season/time of day to ride: weekdays
Points of interest: Jenkins Sheep camp, picnic areas, bird and wildlife viewing
Accommodations and services: 3 campgrounds around Lake Davis, all services in Portola
Supplemental maps or other information: USGS topos for Grizzly Valley and Crocker Mountain

GETTING THERE
From Sacramento, drive north 56 miles on State Highway 99 to Oroville, then take State Highway 70 through Quincy and Blairsden to Portola. Turn left onto County Road 126 (Lake Davis West Street) and drive approximately 7 miles north to Lake Davis Dam. Park at the information kiosk.

IN THE SADDLE
This is a reasonably flat, easy loop around Lake Davis that makes a great family outing. Vehicle traffic may be heavy on portions of the route during summer weekends, so you might want to plan a family tour for a weekday. Throw in camping at one of the three large, well-maintained campgrounds—Grizzly, Grasshopper Flat, and Lightning Tree—and you have the makings of a fine trip. (Note that all three campgrounds are situated on the east side of the lake.)

The Lake Davis Recreation Area is one of the most popular sections of the Plumas National Forest, a region clearly oriented to recreation. Lake Davis is well known for its trout fishing, as are many of the other lakes and streams in the area. At nearly 6,000 feet, Lake Davis sits on the edge of a high desert in the shadow of Smith Peak to the southwest (elevation 7,688 feet).

The directions for the ride around the lake are straightforward. From the parking area at the dam travel 1.7 miles west on County Road 126 (Lake Davis Road) to the junction with Forest Service Road 24N10. Turn right onto Forest Service Road 24N10 and ride for just over 8 miles, until you reach the junction with County Road 112 (Beckwourth–

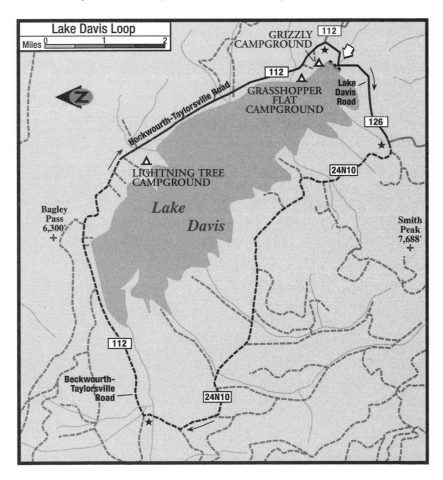

Taylorsville Road). Turn right onto County Road 112 and continue south and east around the lake. Approximately 0.5 mile after you pass the Grizzly Campground turn south onto County Road 126, which will take you back to the dam.

Big Grizzly Creek, which flows out of Lake Davis, feeds the middle fork of the Feather River. El Rio de las Plumas (Spanish for the river of the feathers) was the name Captain Luis Arguello and his band of explorers gave the river when they came upon its lower regions in 1820 and found it strewn with wildfowl feathers. Today, the Feather River is a designated National Wild and Scenic River.

James P. Beckwourth opened up this region in 1850 by discovering a low pass to the east that is the lowest entrance into the state north of the desert gateways in southern California. Beckwourth was the son of a Revolutionary War officer and a slave mother. With his dark skin and long braids, dressed in leather jacket and moccasins, and riding bareback, he made a memorable figure. The town that bears his name is 6 miles to the southeast of Lake Davis, and the pass he opened lies another 15 miles to the east on State Route 70.

Directly to the south of Lake Davis is Portola, an early lumbering and railroad center. Here the most popular attraction is the Portola Railroad Museum, well signed from Highway 70 and definitely worth a visit when you are in the area. Its collection includes many already-restored items, plus a good many pieces under restoration. The museum is an all-volunteer effort sponsored by the Feather River Rail Society. For more information, call (916) 832-4131.

RIDE GUIDE

    0.0 From the Lake Davis Dam parking lot, ride west on County Road 126 (Lake Davis Road).

★   1.7 Turn right onto FR 24N10.

★   9.8 Turn right onto CR112 (Beckwourth-Taylorsville Road).

★ 17.9 Turn right onto CR 126 (Lake Davis Road)

   18.4 Lake Davis Dam. End of ride.

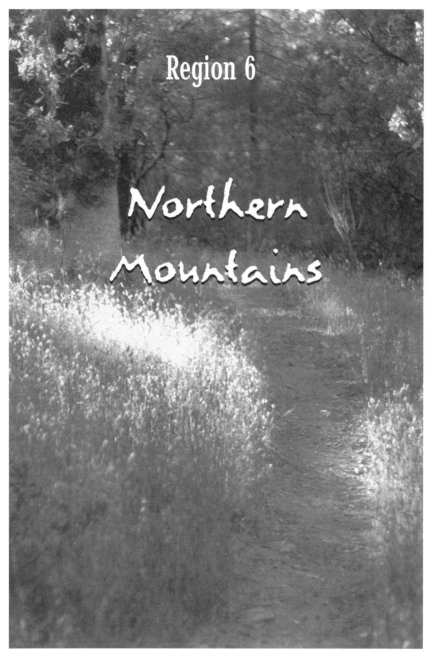

Region 6

Northern Mountains

A nice cool path beckons cyclists. (photo by John Stein)

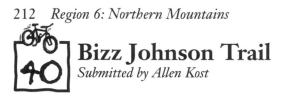

Bizz Johnson Trail
Submitted by Allen Kost

This easy ride along a rail-trail conversion is complete with tunnels and wonderful views along the Susan River.

Type of ride: mountain bike
Starting point: Susanville
Finishing point: same
Distance: 50.9 miles
Level of difficulty: easy
General terrain: flat to gently climbing railroad grade
Traffic conditions: nonexistent
Estimated riding time: 3 to 5 hours
Best season/time of day to ride: spring through fall
Points of interest: Susan River Canyon; railroad tunnels; West-wood park
Accommodations and services: food and water in Susanville and Westwood; camping at Goumaz and at nearby Milford

GETTING THERE

Susanville is in northeastern California, near the Nevada border, on US Highway 395. From the I-5 corridor, take State Highway 36 east from Red Bluff for 115 miles. In Susanville, exit onto North Lassen Street and go approximately 0.5 mile to the well-marked Bizz Johnson Trailhead.

IN THE SADDLE

The directions for this ride are easy. Nearly the entire ride follows a rail-trail conversion along what was once the Fernley and Lassen Branch Line of the Southern Pacific Railroad, built in 1914. You will wind along the Susan River Canyon and cycle through two tunnels, which add to the fun.

The whole round trip between Westwood and Susanville is about 51 miles. The actual rail trail is just over 25 miles; the final 5 miles are on County A21 into the small town of Westwood. In Westwood there are a park and an information kiosk, plus 25-foot high carved redwood statues of Paul Bunyan and his faithful companion, Babe the blue ox.

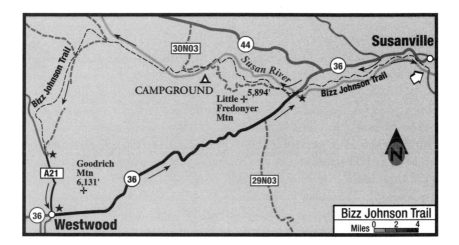

How did two characters from upper Midwest folklore make it all the way to California? Simple: The lumber mill that was served by the Fernley and Lassen Branch was called the Paul Bunyan Lumber Company.

You can make this ride any length you want by pedaling toward Westwood until you have seen enough (some think the first 6 miles out of Susanville are the most scenic). Then turn around and hit the higher gears going back to Susanville. It is not exactly a swift downhill, but pedaling will definitely be easier. You will gain about 1,200 feet over the 30 miles between Susanville and Westwood, which works out to about a 2 percent grade.

There is a campground on the Bizz Johnson Trail at Goumaz, which is accessible by car. From Susanville, proceed west up Main Street and onto State Highway 36. Turn right onto State Highway 44 and proceed 6.5 miles. Then turn left onto a dirt road and left again at the sign to Goumaz. At about 2 miles, cross the Bizz Johnson Trail. On the other side of the trail is a small campground on the right. Bring food and water.

RIDE GUIDE
     0.0 Ride west onto Bizz Johnson Trail.
★ 25.4 Turn left onto County Road A21.
★ 29.9 Turn left onto SR 36.
★ 45.9 Turn right back onto Bizz Johnson Trail.
     50.9 Susanville. End of ride.

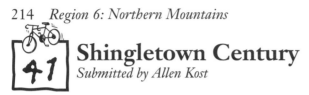

Shingletown Century

Submitted by Allen Kost

Here is a good test to see if you can ride 100 miles in a day, one of those challenges many cyclists like to put themselves up against. You will get scenic views of the Sacramento Valley, plus you will visit Lassen Volcanic National Park.

Type of ride: road bike
Starting point: near Shingletown
Finishing point: same
Distance: 100 miles
Level of difficulty: hard
General terrain: mountainous
Traffic conditions: vary; heaviest on state highways and within Lassen Volcanic National Park
Estimated riding time: 8 to12 hours (get an early start)
Best season/time of day to ride: June through October
Points of interest: Lassen Volcanic National Park
Accommodations and services: small stores in communities along the way
Supplemental maps or other information: AAA Northeastern California map

GETTING THERE
From the I-5 corridor, take State Highway 44 east from Redding for 22 miles to Black Butte Road, 6.5 miles west of Shingletown. Turn right onto Black Butte Road and immediately left into a Park 'n' Ride lot.

IN THE SADDLE
In planning for this ride, add a third water bottle and do not forget to take $5 to get into the park entrance. From the parking lot, go south

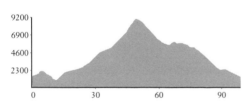

on Black Butte Road, which becomes Wildcat Road (do not turn right onto Wildcat for the last 8.5 miles to the junction with Manton Road. Turn right onto Manton

Road for 0.5 mile, then left on Lanes Valley Road to its end at State Highway 36. (A short detour to the right onto State Highway 36 and then a left on Plum Creek Road will take you to Paynes Creek and a small store where you might get water, but do not count on the store being open.) From Lanes Valley Road, turn left onto State Highway 36 and ride 20 miles to the town of Mineral. There is a small store here for food and water.

Continue on State Highway 36 for another 4 miles to the turnoff for Lassen National Volcanic Park and turn left (north) onto State Highway 89 (Lassen Loop Road). This road is closed from the first good snowfall until May or early June most years.

In 5 miles, you will reach the entrance station to the park. Water and rest rooms are available, and there may be food at a chalet just past the entrance station.

Climb 7.5 miles to the summit of Lassen Loop Road, at 8,512 feet. You can lock your bike and hike the trail to the peak if you have the time and stamina to do it. Do not ride or carry your bike on the trail to the peak—it is strictly prohibited.

Continue another 21 miles to the junction with State Highway 44. As you near the junction, there are rest rooms and water in a rest stop

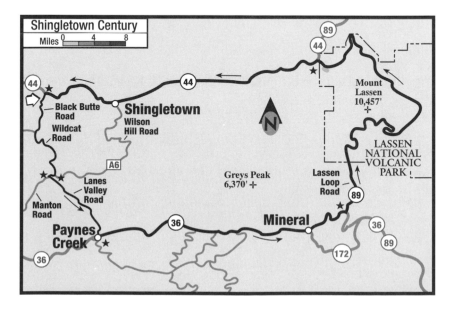

near the highway. Turn left (west) onto State Highway 44 for the 25-mile return ride to the Park 'n' Ride lot. The highway is particularly narrow east of Viola, but at least you will be going downhill at that point. There are stores in Shingletown and near the parking lot.

The total climbing on this ride is 10,000 feet, which always adds interest to a century ride.

RIDE GUIDE

  0.0 From Park 'n' Ride on Black Butte Road, ride south on Black Butte Road.

  4.2 Route becomes Wildcat Road.

★ 8.4 Turn right onto Manton Road.

★ 8.9 Turn left onto Lanes Valley Road.

★ 16.8 Paynes Creek. Turn left onto SR 36.

 36.6 Mineral. Continue on SR 36.

★ 40.6 Turn left onto SR 89 (Lassen Loop Road).

 45.4 Lassen National Volcanic Park entrance station.

 52.9 Summit. Continue on SR 89 (Lassen Loop Road).

★ 66.2 Turn left onto SR 44.

 74.2 Shingletown.

★ 99.8 Turn left onto Black Butte Road.

 100.0 Park 'n' Ride. End of ride.

Lake Almanor–Warner Valley

Submitted by Roy Berridge

To recreationists, Lake Almanor, a human-made lake in the Lassen National Forest, is well-known for its fishing, water skiing, and sailing. After you have done this loop, you will wonder why more bicyclists do not seem to know about it.

Type of ride: road bike
Starting point: Chester
Finishing point: same
Distance: 60 miles
Level of difficulty: easy; only two steep, short hills

General terrain: moderately rolling
Traffic conditions: light to moderate on shoreline roads
Estimated riding time: 4 to 5 hours
Best season/time of day to ride: late May through September
Points of interest: views of Mount Lassen and Lake Almanor
Accommodations and services: all services in Chester
Supplemental maps or other information: Chester–Lake Almanor
   Chamber of Commerce, P.O. Box 1198, Chester, CA 96020, (916)
   258-2426

GETTING THERE
This relatively easy loop route begins and ends in the small northern
California mountain community of Chester. Chester is located 72 miles
east of Red Bluff (on I-5) along State Highway 36 and 77 miles northeast of Chico on State Highway 32.

IN THE SADDLE
Chester is surrounded by the Lassen National Forest and large private
timberland holdings. At an elevation of 4,531 feet, Chester's location
in the southern portion of the Cascade Mountain Range places it among

Mount Lassen as seen from Lee Camp (photo by Roy Berridge)

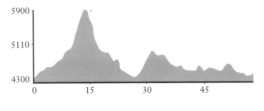

mixed conifer forests of pine, fir, and incense cedar. Chester is the only full-service community near Lassen National Volcanic Park, located about 30 miles west of the town on State Highway 36.

Directly south of Chester is Lake Almanor, a human-made lake constructed in 1905. The lake is owned by Pacific Gas and Electric Company (PG&E) as part of its hydroelectric development of California's Feather River.

Due to the higher elevations involved, much of the Lake Almanor route is snowed in from December through March. The best time for this ride is from late May through September.

This ride is comprised of two segments, each starting and ending in Chester. The Warner Valley out-and-back segment is approximately 28 miles in length (the second half is a gentle downhill return to Chester). The Lake Almanor segment is a loop, just over 32 miles in length. With only short stops along the way, the Warner Valley segment can be ridden in about 2 hours; the Lake Almanor segment will require between 2.5 and 3.0 hours. Because of the beautiful scenery and sites that beckon as suitable lunch or rest stops, riders should allow more time if possible. The more leisurely cyclist or family could use Chester as a base camp and ride the two sections on consecutive days.

WARNER VALLEY SEGMENT

Beginning at the Chester Fire Station, at Main Street and Feather River Drive, go north on Feather River Drive. This is also known locally as Drakesbad Road. The ride out of "old town" is on a straight, level road lined with pine and cottonwood trees.

At a fork in the road, turn left toward Drakesbad, a guest ranch in the southeastern corner of Lassen National Park. The road is paved, usually lightly trafficked, with a few gently rolling hills. A couple of miles and a steeper hill or two will bring you to Lassen National Forest. You will travel through some clearcut areas, interspersed with old-growth forests of Jeffrey and lodgepole pine. Deer are plentiful, and you might see the occasional bear.

Just after the High Bridge Campground (USFS), tackle the steepest hill on this loop; it may give your lungs a workout, but it is only 0.2 mile long, so it will not be too much of a strain. After reaching the top, the remaining 20 miles are easy.

At a second fork, take the right-hand turn, again continuing toward Drakesbad. (If looking for a campground, take the fork to the left 2.5 miles to Domingo Springs, USFS. The pavement ends at the campground. You will have an easy retrace to the route in the morning.)

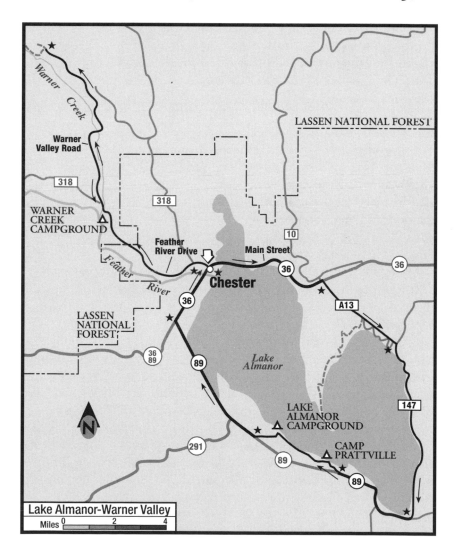

Approximately 3 miles past the fork, cross Warner Creek. To the left (north) is Mount Harkness, in Lassen National Park. During the fall, bright yellow leaves adorn the aspens in the meadow.

In another 3 miles, you will have the best view of Mount Lassen (elevation 10,457 feet) on the ride. The site is known as Lee's Camp, where the old homestead for the Lee Ranch formerly stood. From here, climb gradually to the end of the outbound route, where the pavement ends.

Now comes the really easy part. Since you have been gradually climbing during most of the ride—gaining about 900 feet between Chester and the turnaround point—the return ride to Chester is mostly downhill. If you are going to ride the second portion, return to the Chester Fire Station.

LAKE ALMANOR SEGMENT

This segment follows paved county and state highways around Lake Almanor. At the Chester Fire Station, turn left onto Main Street (State Highway 36) and go east along Main Street through "old town." Just after leaving Chester, you will get your first view of Lake Almanor on the right and Mount Lassen on the left (to the north). Cross a small arm of the lake on a causeway and begin a gradual climb up the Johnson Grade. There is a rest area at the top of the grade.

Five miles into the ride, turn right (south) off State Highway 36 onto County Highway A13. A couple of gradual climbs and fast descents will bring you to the small community of Hamilton Branch (some services).

Another right-hand turn onto County Highway 147 will take you toward Greenville and along Lake Almanor's east shore, with Mount Lassen standing as a backdrop behind frequent views of the lake. Traffic is moderate, and you may encounter an occasional log truck or chip van. You will hear them coming in plenty of time to clear the road.

Turning right again onto State Highway 89 will take you on the western leg of the loop and back toward Chester. (State Highway 89 is also signed for Red Bluff, beyond Chester.) Cross the spillway of Lake Almanor and pass a couple of campgrounds maintained by PG&E. About 3 miles past the spillway, turn right off State Highway 89 toward the lake onto an unmarked county road; watch for an old cemetery on your left shortly before you get to Prattville. The traffic is very light on

View of Lake Almanor from the spillway (photo by Roy Berridge)

this section. Camp Prattville has a popular small cafe. Near this point is the original site of Prattville, which was inundated when the lake was constructed. You will pass Lake Almanor Campground shortly before rejoining State Highway 89. This road will take you back to State Highway 36 into Chester.

Note: The Almanor Lake segment is one of the rides sponsored annually by the Almanor Wheelpeople, a bicycle club. It is known as the Mile High Hundred and is held mid-June.

RIDE GUIDE
Warner Valley Segment
0.0 From corner of Main Street and Feather River Drive in Chester, ride north on Feather River Drive.
★ 0.6 At fork, turn left to continue on Feather River Drive (Warner Valley Road).
3.6 Lassen National Forest.
6.1 At fork, bear right to continue on Feather River Drive (Warner Valley Road).
7.2 Warner Creek Campground.
9.1 Cross Warner Creek.
★ 13.4 End of pavement. Turn around and ride back way you came.
26.8 Chester. End of segment.

Lake Almanor Segment
★ 26.8 Turn left onto Main Street (SR 36).
★ 31.8 Turn right onto County Road A13.

★ 35.7 Turn right onto County Highway 147.
★ 43.2 Turn right onto SR 89.
★ 46.7 Turn right onto unnamed county road.
   48.7 Camp Prattville.
   50.0 Lake Almanor Campground.
★ 50.7 Turn right onto SR 89.
★ 56.3 Turn right onto SR 36.
   58.7 Chester. End of ride.

Clikapudi Trail
Submitted by John Stein

This easy-to-moderate mountain bike loop takes you along and above Shasta Lake. You will also cruise through a protected archeological site.

Type of ride: mountain bike
Starting point: Clikapudi Trailhead at Jones Valley Boat Ramp, Lake Shasta
Finishing point: same
Distance: 7.25 miles
Level of difficulty: easy to moderate
General terrain: varies with some steep but short climbs
Traffic conditions: very light; short section of jeep road may have traffic
Estimated riding time: 1 to 2 hours
Best season/time of day to ride: often open year-round
Points of interest: views of Lake Shasta; archeological site
Accommodations and services: none; camping nearby
Supplemental maps or other information: Shasta Trinity National Forest visitors map, available from Shasta National Recreation Area, 2400 Washington Street, Redding, CA 96001, (916) 246-5222

GETTING THERE
The Clikapudi Trail is 16 miles northeast of Redding on Shasta Lake. From the I-5 corridor, 5 miles north of Redding, take the Oasis Road exit east. Follow the National Forest signs to Old Oregon Trail, Bear Mountain Road, and the village of Jones Valley. The trailhead is 2 miles

The trail as it skirts around Lake Shasta (photo by John Stein)

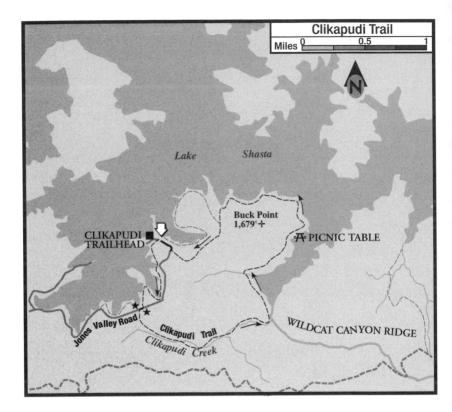

farther at the Jones Valley Boat Ramp parking lot. There is a $5 fee for parking in this lot. You can park for no charge along the access road.

IN THE SADDLE

The boat ramp parking lot is your starting point. Ignore the obvious trailhead sign—this is where you will exit the trail. Find the southeast corner of the parking lot and enter the trail there.

With 365 miles of shoreline, Lake Shasta is California's largest reservoir. The high fill levels occur in May and June; by October, the reservoir is drawn down to expose red banks and beaches.

The first portion of the Clikapudi Trail is very level and provides access to the Lake Shasta shoreline at four points. You will twist in and out of coves and cross small seasonal streams. At about 1.6 miles, watch for a critical left turn. Follow this fork for 1.8 miles, climbing to the paved road. Turn right onto the road for 0.1 mile and watch for an unmarked trailhead on your left. Shift into your granny gear before you attack this 0.25-mile climb up switchbacks. Use the panorama of Shasta Lake as an excuse for a breather at the top of the climb. Bald eagles frequent this area year-round.

Start down the ridge into the next drainage. After a tricky switchback, you will get a nice downhill to mile 2.8. The hidden valley meadow you have entered is a protected archeological site of the Wintu tribe and older cultures dating back thousands of years. This is a very special place.

A jeep road intersects the Clikapudi Trail at mile 2.9 and then winds along with your trail, crossing it occasionally. At 3.3 miles, keep left of the creek and leave any vehicle traffic behind. At 3.7 miles, there is a distinct change in the flora as the shady side of the ridge fosters more pines and firs, rather than the valley oaks you have been riding through.

Once you are back at the lake, the undergrowth becomes more dense, sometimes pushing onto the trail. As the trail opens again, there are a few rocky sections where the less experienced rider may choose to dismount. At mile 5, there are picnic tables where you can take a breather or have a lunch with Shasta Lake as a backdrop.

A footbridge along the trail (photo by John Stein)

The next mile rolls along the shoreline before climbing out of a gully for 0.25 mile up to a lovely oak knoll. Avoid the shortcut trail and keep to the right to wander through this nice open space.

Your final trail section is a quick downhill that will drop you rapidly to the water's edge. There is only a 0.2-mile climb back to the parking lot to finish the 7.25-mile loop, so you might as well take advantage of a last chance for a dip in a cove. Summer temperatures can exceed 100 degrees here, so this may be a welcome choice.

RIDE GUIDE

    0.0 From parking lot at Clikapudi Trailhead, find southeast corner of lot and enter trail there.

    1.6 Turn left.

★   1.8 Turn right onto paved road.

★   1.9 Turn left onto unmarked trail.

    2.9 Intersection with jeep road. Continue on trail.

    3.3 Keep left of creek.

    5.0 Picnic table.

    7.0 Lakeshore.

    7.2 Parking lot. End of ride.

The Three Shastas
Submitted by Allen Kost

This short loop ride is named for its viewpoints of Shasta Dam, Shasta Lake, and Mount Shasta in the distance.

Type of ride: road bike
Starting point: City of Shasta Lake
Finishing point: same
Distance: 12 miles
Level of difficulty: easy to moderate, with one 2-mile climb
General terrain: hilly
Traffic conditions: mostly light traffic on two-lane roads with no shoulders; possibly congested in area of the dam and boat ramp
Estimated riding time: 1.5 to 2.0 hours

Best season/time of day to ride: early in the mornings in the summer and later in the day during the winter; route generally open year-round

Points of interest: the Three Shastas: the dam, the peak, and the lake

Accommodations and services: no campgrounds at this location; food services in the community of Shasta Lake and nearby towns

Supplemental maps or other information: AAA Map for Northwestern California

GETTING THERE

From the I-5 corridor, 6 miles north of Redding, exit onto State Highway 151 to the west. Go to the city of Shasta Lake on Shasta Dam Boulevard. On-street parking is available there.

IN THE SADDLE

Leave the city of Shasta Lake on Shasta Dam Boulevard (State Highway 151). Ride 3 miles to the junction with County Road A18, also called Lake Boulevard. Cross Lake Boulevard and continue on Shasta Dam Boulevard for another 4 miles to Shasta Dam. After crossing Lake Boulevard, you will have a 2-mile climb, followed by a 2-mile descent to Shasta Dam.

After touring the dam area, continue past the traffic circle on A18 (Lake Boulevard), where you will pass rest rooms. Water is also available at the dam. (To add some miles and a 600-foot climb, you can ride to the base of the dam and pick up the out-and-back road to the powerhouse area.)

Leaving the dam, climb a 0.5-mile hill past the turnoff for the Clikapudi boat ramp. Then you will get a 1.5-mile downhill to the junction with State Highway 151 (Shasta Dam Boulevard).

Turn left onto Shasta Dam Boulevard and ride the 3 miles back to where you parked.

Shasta Lake is California's largest reservoir and a popular boating and recreation area for

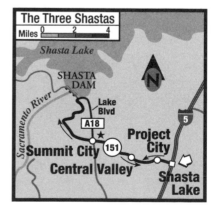

northern Californians. The lake is highest in May and June; by October of each year, the waters have been drawn down to where there are more beaches available.

Two of the primary draws of this ride are the tour of Shasta Dam and the views of Mount Shasta (elevation 14,162 feet) approximately 50 miles to the north.

RIDE GUIDE

     0.0 From on-street parking, ride west on SR 151.

★   3.0 Cross Lake Boulevard (County Road A18).

     7.0 Shasta Dam.

     7.5 Continue past traffic circle on County Road A18.

★   9.0 Turn left onto SR 151.

  12.0 Parking. End of ride.

Index

About the Contributers

Steven Anderson has been cycling all of his life. Now that his children are grown, he has even more time to bicycle. Steven, a member of Adventure Cycling for the past three years, submitted the *Davis Romp*, a loop ride beginning and ending in California's "bicycle town" of Davis.

Nan Baker has toured extensively throughout North America, riding across Canada and the United States from California to Alaska. Nan, a member of Adventure Cycling for sixteen years, submitted the *American River Ride*.

Alan and **Jane Baron** enjoy cycling with their children. One of their favorite rides is the *Occidental Loop*, with its coastline and the mountain scenery. Alan and Jane have been members of Adventure Cycling for ten years.

Roy Berridge, a veteran bicyclist, has been a member of Adventure Cycling for one year. Roy submitted the *Lake Almanor–Warner Valley* ride, one of his favorites because of the two different terrains encountered on the ride.

Alan Bloom just completed his first self-contained cross-country bicycle trip. Alan, a member of Adventure Cycling for one year, submitted three rides for this book: *Vineyard Loop, St. Helena,* and *Boont Talk Ride.*

Daniel L. Cikuth, a member of Adventure Cycling for one year, loves a little different style of bike touring, as evidenced by his *Slammin' Salmon Tour.*

Andrew Davidson loves getting out on his road bike as often as possible, and he is trying to commute more often using his bike. Andrew, who has been a member of Adventure Cycling for three years, submitted the *Mount Tam Climb*, one of his favorite road rides.

Curt Ferguson, who has been a member of Adventure Cycling for one year, submitted the *Chimney Rock* ride, one of his favorite road rides. Curt loves both mountain and road biking, with an emphasis on endurance mountain biking, particularly the Leadville 100.

Don Gray submitted one of his favorite "neighborhood" rides, the *Berkeley Loop*. Don is a life member of Adventure Cycling and enjoys touring throughout California.

Jim Haagen-Smit and his wife, Cathy, are experienced tandem cyclists. Their mountain and road tandems take them riding all over the globe. Jim submitted the *Mount Lola Peak* and *Bullards Bar Loop* rides. Jim and Cathy are active with many bicycle advocacy groups, and are dedicated year-round bike commuters.

Stan Hansen has been bike touring for more than twenty years. Stan, a member of Adventure Cycling for just over a year, submitted both the *Avenue of the Giants* and *Oakdale to Yosemite* rides.

James L. Hardy, who submitted the *Gold Lake Ride*, enjoys touring on his tandem with his wife. They have been cycling for ten years and recently did a tour in Europe. They have been Adventure Cycling members for two years.

Scott Harriger, an avid mountain biker, has been a member of Adventure Cycling for one year. Scott submitted the *Wilder Ridge Loop* ride, which takes you through his favorite area in northern California to ride.

Karl Kneip, an adventure Cycling member for ten years, submitted the *Duncan Mills Ramble*. Karl loves reading group bike rides over the golden hills of Sonoma County.

Allen Kost, who has been cycling for ten years, submitted the *Whiskeytown Lake*, *Lake Davis*, *Bizz Johnson*, *Shingletown*, *Three Shastas*, and *Redding to Ferndale* rides. Allen has been an Adventure Cycling member for six years and enjoys touring the Oregon coast with his wife, Kathy.

Roger McGehee, a new Adventure Cycling member, is an intermediate mountain biker with a passion for single-track. Roger also keeps fellow riders abreast of single-track rides in his area, which he puts on his Web page. He submitted the *Middle Ridge Loop* and the *Downieville Downhill* rides.

Jill McIntire, a member of Adventure Cycling for ten years, submitted the *Unknown Coast* ride. Jill has been cycling for many years and this is one of her favorites.

Ed McLaughlin, the past owner of a bicycle messenger service, is currently the general manager of a cycling club. He submitted one of the club's rides, the *Chico-Durham Loop*. Ed has been a member of Adventure Cycling for one year and has been "car free" for fifteen years.

Emmett Maguire is a Navy veteran and retired printer who, among his many cycle touring experiences, has several self-contained cross-country bike trips to his credit. Emmett has been a member of Adventure Cycling for eleven years; he submitted the *Tomales Bay Loop* ride.

Jean O'Brien is a retired school teacher who has been a member of Adventure Cycling for four years. She has completed several self-contained tours around the country. When she's not cycling, Jean instructs a bicycling class geared toward seniors at a local community college. She submitted the *Knights Ferry* ride.

William Paxson is primarily a road-bike cyclist who has toured in Washington, Oregon, and Utah. He has been a member of Adventure Cycling for four years. Bill says that all of his bikes are equipped with "grandpa gears," which assist mightily in getting him through the ride he submitted: the *Eldorado Climb*.

Richard Peters, who has been cycling for many years, submitted the *Sutter Buttes* ride, one of his favorites. He has been a member of Adventure Cycling for one year.

Earle Reynolds, who has been cycling since the early 1970s, submitted the *Dutch Flat* ride. Earle and his wife, Laura, have toured throughout the country, and Earle continues to lead club rides and weekend tours. Earle and Laura have been members of Adventure Cycling for ten years.

Al Schoenemann enjoys cycling both of the routes he submitted: the *Sutter Creek* and *Ione Loop* rides. Al has been a member of Adventure Cycling for four years.

John Stein, who started bicycling by touring California's Eastern Sierra in 1972, submitted the *South Fork Trail* and *Clikapudi Trail* rides. He currently manages a bike shop between weekends. John has been an Adventure Cycling member for three years.

Kurt Sunderbruch, a member of Adventure Cycling for two years, submitted the *Lincoln Loop*, one of his favorite "after-work" rides.

Marianne Tamm is a recent member of Adventure Cycling who is not new to the sport: she has toured extensively, including a three-month tour through Europe. Marianne submitted the *Pescadero Loop* ride.

David and **Kristina Vandershaf** have been Adventure Cycling members for four years, and enjoy all types of touring for both road and mountain bikes. They submitted the *Klamath Forest Ride* and the *Nevada City Ramble*.

Bob Wall, a member of Adventure Cycling for two years, submitted the *Clear Lake to the Coast* ride. Bob tries to bicycle as much as possible when he can get away from running his business with his wife, Jeanne.

Wally West, who submitted the *Garberville Trek* ride, has been a member of Adventure Cycling for three years. Wally enjoys getting away with his B.O.B. trailer for a few days of self-contained mountain bike touring.

Sandy Zirulnik moved by bicycle from Michigan to California in 1970, and has been pedaling ever since. He has been a member of Adventure Cycling for one year. Sandy enjoys both on- and off-road touring; he submitted the *Bovine Bakery Ride*.

OTHER TITLES YOU MAY ENJOY FROM THE MOUNTAINEERS:

ADVENTURE CYCLING IN MICHIGAN: Selected On- and Off-Road Rides, *The Adventure Cycling Association*
Premier cycling organization presents the 44 best bike trips in Michigan for mountain bikers and on-road cyclists.

BICYCLING COAST TO COAST: A Complete Route Guide, Virginia to Oregon, *Donna Lynn Ikenberry*
The definitive coast-to-coast biking guide; the route covers 10 states and more than 4,000 miles, and is divided into 77 daily segments which can be combined to bike the complete route or used as guides to shorter rides.

BICYCLING THE ATLANTIC COAST: A Complete Route Guide, Florida to Maine, *Donna Lynn Ikenberry*
The only complete touring guide to the East Coast; covers road conditions, where to buy provisions, camping, and points of interest.

BICYCLING THE PACIFIC COAST, Second Edition: A Complete Route Guide, Canada to Mexico, *Tom Kirkendall & Vicky Spring*
Fully-detailed, authoritative guide to pedaling the West Coast presents comprehensive information on road conditions, points of interest, and more.

BICYCLING THE BACKROADS AROUND PUGET SOUND, Fourth Edition, *Erin & Bill Woods*
BICYCLING THE BACKROADS OF NORTHWEST OREGON, Second Edition, *Erin & Bill Woods*
BICYCLING THE BACKROADS OF SOUTHWEST WASHINGTON, Third Edition, *Erin & Bill Woods*

BIKING THE GREAT NORTHWEST: 20 Tours in Washington, Oregon, Idaho, and Montana, *Jean Henderson*
Collection of multi-day tours, many of them loops, for great Northwest cycling vacations. Includes mileage logs and notes on terrain, history, scenic highlights, and cycling smarts.

MOUNTAIN BIKE ADVENTURES IN WASHINGTON'S NORTH CASCADES AND OLYMPICS, Second Edition, *Tom Kirkendall*
60 of the best off-road bike trails from Interstate 90 north to the Canadian border, plus the Olympics.

MOUNTAIN BIKE ADVENTURES IN WASHINGTON'S SOUTH CASCADES AND PUGET SOUND, Second Edition, *Tom Kirkendall*
Covers the region from Interstate 90 south to the Columbia River, offering trails to suit both novice and experienced mountain bikers.

MOUNTAIN BIKE EMERGENCY REPAIR, *Tim Toyoshima*
Pocket-sized handbook shows how to perform temporary trailside repairs with few or no tools, and then make permanent repairs with proper tools.

THE MOUNTAINEERS, founded in 1906, is a nonprofit outdoor activity and conservation club, whose mission is "to explore, study, preserve, and enjoy the natural beauty of the outdoors. . . . " Based in Seattle, Washington, the club is now the third-largest such organization in the United States, with 15,000 members and five branches throughout Washington State.

The Mountaineers sponsors both classes and year-round outdoor activities in the Pacific Northwest, which include hiking, mountain climbing, ski-touring, snowshoeing, bicycling, camping, kayaking and canoeing, nature study, sailing, and adventure travel. The club's conservation division supports environmental causes through educational activities, sponsoring legislation, and presenting informational programs. All club activities are led by skilled, experienced volunteers, who are dedicated to promoting safe and responsible enjoyment and preservation of the outdoors.

If you would like to participate in these organized outdoor activities or the club's programs, consider a membership in The Mountaineers. For information and an application, write or call The Mountaineers, Club Headquarters, 300 Third Avenue West, Seattle, Washington 98119, (206) 284-6310; e-mail: clubmail@mountaineers.org

The Mountaineers Books, an active, nonprofit publishing program of the club, produces guidebooks, instructional texts, historical works, natural history guides, and works on environmental conservation. All books produced by The Mountaineers are aimed at fulfilling the club's mission.

Send or call for our catalog of more than 300 outdoor titles:

 The Mountaineers Books
1001 SW Klickitat Way, Suite 201
Seattle, WA 98134
1-800-553-4453 / e-mail: mbooks@mountaineers.org